THE
MISSING
PIECE

THE MISSING PIECE

Finding the Better Part of Me:
A Love Journey

ROB HILL SR.

WITH JAS WATERS

ATRIA BOOKS

New York   London   Toronto   Sydney   New Delhi

ATRIA
BOOKS

An Imprint of Simon & Schuster, Inc.
1230 Avenue of the Americas
New York, NY 10020

First Atria Books hardcover edition June 2018

ATRIA BOOKS and colophon are trademarks of Simon & Schuster, Inc.

For information about special discounts for bulk purchases, please contact Simon
& Schuster Special Sales at 1-866-506-1949 or business@simonandschuster.com.

The Simon & Schuster Speakers Bureau can bring authors to your live event. For
more information, or to book an event, contact the Simon & Schuster Speakers
Bureau at 1-866-248-3049 or visit our website at www.simonspeakers.com.

Interior design by Joy O'Meara

Manufactured in the United States of America

10 9 8 7 6 5 4 3 2 1

Library of Congress Cataloging-in-Publication Data

Names: Hillman, Robert Brandyn, 1987– author. | Waters, Jas, author.
Title: The missing piece : finding the better part of me, a love journey /
Rob Hill, Sr. with Jas Waters.
Description: New York : Atria Books, [2018]
Identifiers: LCCN 2018005011 (print) | LCCN 2018015804 (ebook) |
ISBN 9781476791692 (Ebook) | ISBN 9780671732318 (hardcover) |
ISBN 9781501140501 (tradepaper) | ISBN 9781476791685
Subjects: LCSH: Self-actualization (Psychology)
Classification: LCC BF637.S4 (ebook) | LCC BF637.S4 H546 2018 (print) |
DDC 158.092—dc23
LC record available at https://lccn.loc.gov/2018005011

ISBN 978-1-4767-9168-5
ISBN 978-1-4767-9169-2 (ebook)

This book is dedicated to my son, Robert Jr.
Always trust God. Always choose Love.
Always believe in yourself.

CONTENTS

CONTENTS

Walk with Me

This is no fairy tale. Within the pages of this book you will find no mention of glass slippers, princes, fairy godmothers, sleeping beauties, or evil witches. A whale swallows no one, and a woodcarver's puppet, magically sprung to life, won't cry as his nose grows with each lie. You won't find any of that here.

There is only me.

I'll start by saying I'm no expert at life. My story is about a misguided young man dancing in the gray and choosing to live dangerously in the middle. I am a student of love. This book is about the period in my life when I was most broken, unable to gather all the pieces, much less put them back together. I've heard that "not all those who wander are lost," but not all who are lost even know they're wandering. I ran, mostly from the truth, but occasionally from myself. I was a runner by nature, and usually without a destination in mind.

Before getting too deep into my story, I want you to know five specific things about me:

1. I grew up as a military dependent, and our family traveled often.

When I turned seven, the world as I knew it changed. My mother met Frank Anderson III on a blind date at a Ruby Tuesday in Raleigh, North Carolina. They were friends at first. Both were young divorced parents; Frank a father of one, Frank IV, and my mother, Monique, had two: my older sister, Elise, and me. They were careful about how their relationship progressed. Frank was a military man and he had a very dependable and trusting way about him. Nine months after their blind date, they married July 1, 1995, in Chesapeake, Virginia. They had my younger sisters Brianna and Ahmore a few years later, in 1998 and 1999. Up until this point, Chesapeake in the Hampton Roads area of Virginia was my home, but after that day my definition of home was never the same.

Starting a new school happens to most children three to four times throughout their lives. Preschool, elementary, middle, then high school are the usual transitions. But when you're a military family like we were, you have to get used to relocating regularly. And with that comes new environments, schedules, social circles, and new schools. I was uncomfortable each time I had to start a new school, and the worst transitions often came in the middle of the school year. The best way to describe it is that it's like walking into a room full of people who have known one another for years and everyone quiets to a hush as you take your seat. Nobody knows what to say, so they just watch and observe you. Now imagine having to do that as a child; then imagine that child having to do that eleven times.

There's a certain rapport children build with one another that allows them to become comfortable. Over time you learn which friend is great for playing basketball, which friend's mom buys all the good snacks, which always has the latest video games, who has the best manners so my mom doesn't mind if he sleeps over. As a military child, the time needed to get comfortable in a new environment was rarely afforded. Once I got settled and at ease, I knew sooner or later I could be moving. Constantly walking into that room full of people who have known one another their entire lives became my normal. Only it wasn't normal.

The experience at each school meant a lot to me. To give you a sense of just how many schools I attended, I'm listing them below.

- George Washington Primary School (Chesapeake, VA): kindergarten and 1st grade, 1992–1994
- College Park Elementary School (Virginia Beach, VA): 2nd grade, 1994
  The sound of wedding bells ringing. Family moves to North Carolina.

- Millbrook Elementary International Baccalaureate Primary Years Programme Magnet School (Raleigh, NC): 3rd grade, 1995
The sound of relief. Family moves back to Virginia.
- Camelot Elementary School (Chesapeake, VA): 4th grade, 1996
Thinks that this is bullshit but kinda cool at the same time as family moves to California.
- Acacia Baptist Elementary School (Hawthorne, CA): 4th grade, 1996–1997
- White Point Elementary School (San Pedro, CA): 5th grade, 1997–1998
- Richard Henry Dana Middle School (San Pedro, CA): 6th grade, 1998–1999
The sound of crying. A whole lot of crying. Family moves to Germany, but back to Virginia first.
- Hugo A. Owens Middle School (Chesapeake, VA): 7th grade, 1999
- Baumholder American High School (Baumholder, Germany): 7th grade, 2000
If it's starting to feel like a lot, imagine actually doing it.
- Hugo A. Owens Middle School (Chesapeake, VA): 8th grade, 2001
- Baumholder American High School (Baumholder, Germany): 8th and 9th grade, 2001
- Monmouth Regional High School (Tinton Falls, NJ): 10th and 11th grade, 2002–2004
- Deep Creek High School (Chesapeake, VA): 12th grade, 2004–2005

2. I'm a father. I have two dads.

Frank was the most consistent father figure throughout my life. He understood the value of discipline. He was patient. With him I always felt a sense of stability and safety. He was strict but he was a good guy, a man with clear principles. He provided for my sister Elise and me like we were his own. We spent quality family time and every day he made my mom light up with joy. I see how my mother knew Frank would be good for us.

Dana, my biological father, had to be a dad from a distance. I wondered how that affected him, but I also wondered if he really cared about me. I wasn't sure.

At twenty years old, I became a father as well. I'll get more into that later.

3. I am wandering romantic.

Relationships, be they platonic, romantic, or professional, are a big part of our lives.

Many of my adult frustrations and problems began when I traveled the world during my adolescent years. The constant travel and relocation influenced the way I approached relationships. I had to say too many goodbyes sooner than I wanted to. I got accustomed to running from problems rather than ever really solving them. I became a skilled runner whenever I was emotionally overwhelmed. I would hold in my pain and pass off a lot, always pretending as if I was okay. Unlike Frank, I rarely utilized patience or let things play out naturally. Instead,

I looked for the shortcut before time ran out. "New move, clean slate" was my motto. I learned not to spend too much time missing places and people I knew I would never see again. And as I grew older and began searching for fulfillment, I oftentimes found myself coming up short.

4. I'm a proud navy veteran.

The US military legacy is in my family. My mother's father, Papa, retired as a chief in the navy and my dad Frank retired as a colonel in the army. I served four years in the navy before separating. A military career until retirement wasn't something I could commit to.

My decision to enlist in the navy was inspired by my son. More about that later.

5. I believe love is really all that matters.

There comes a time when our actions and desires have to balance out and we must choose the person that we most want to be. This book serves as my opportunity to look back, reflect, and to share the life lessons that helped me decide what kind of person I wanted to be. There is no proven formula for how to live a perfect life. In fact, there is no perfect life. But a fulfilling life is not only real, it's obtainable. Not one of us was cheated in our design, but many of us get lost comparing and competing in areas that we shouldn't. I should know, I was that person. I spent years chasing the idea in my head of who I should become all the while ignoring what life was trying to teach me about who I already was. It wasn't until I made it past my own doubt, fear, and shortcomings that I finally learned to see me. And it took trying to force love into all the wrong relationships before I finally got around to loving myself.

The greatest opponent we face in the game of life is ourselves. We spend hours, days, and years searching for answers to the questions in our heart. But the answer is there. Our full awareness of self, our understanding of purpose, and our appreciation for the power of love are the missing pieces to alleviate the pain so many people feel. It was the answer to the pain I felt.

Some of us go through major life experiences too early and some of us make adult decisions prematurely, like getting married and having children. We do so unaware of how these decisions can follow us for the rest of our lives. The pain of unintended consequences can shift each person's course differently, some for better, others for worse. My "way" was about what was comfortable for me and not necessarily what was best for me.

Through every experience we find a new piece of ourselves. Each day, with each choice we either reaffirm who we are or introduce a new part of who we've become. Growth, joy, and love are things we must choose to continuously welcome in our lives. The spirit of our future depends on our ability to stay open, moldable, and honest. When I look back on my life I don't have any regrets. Through every mistake I've made I've learned many lessons. I was broken and I didn't recognize how low I let myself start to feel, I just know that I felt something was missing from my life. And I had all the wrong ideas of what it was. I thought, if only I had this car, this job, this house, or this woman, then I'd be whole. But with the fulfillment of each thing came more longing. And I am not alone in this. Although this story is mine, the lessons these reflections uncover are meant to help you improve life emotionally, spiritually, and in your relationships. No matter who you are, where you're from, your social status, or political leaning, there's been a point in your life when you felt like something was missing. Like some of the pieces were around, but not enough to add up and get the game going. So I pose the questions:

What will it mean to you to feel whole?
What will finally make you happier?
What can increase your faith?
Will you embrace peace in your relationships?
How will you give your love?

Welcome to *The Missing Piece*. I pray you leave this book with the inspiration to fulfill your purpose in life. And I hope that within these pages you find a reason to love, heal, forgive, and be free. It's time.

Walk with me . . .

CHAPTER ONE

Appearances Ain't Nothin'

Your mother says you can't come home." My dad, Dana, rarely called me so I knew this was serious.

"I'm going to let you stay with me for a little bit, but just until you get a plan."

I didn't like that he thought I needed him. But I also didn't have a plan for where I would be sleeping in a few hours. I listened, he gave me the address, and I told him that I would get a ride to his house. As I mentioned earlier, Dana had to be a dad from a distance and though we had short conversations here and there, we weren't close. He had a spare room just big enough for a twin bed, a desk, and a lamp. After an agreement with his wife, Lynette, they charged me fifty dollars a week to live in it. The idea never occurred to me that this could be an opportunity to get to know my father better. At seventeen, I told myself that I was grown and that I didn't have anything to learn from him now. All I needed was somewhere to place my few belongings, keys to a door I could open when I saw fit, and a bed to crash in when I was tired from doing whatever it was I wanted to do that day.

I undervalued family at that time in my life. I thought to not show emotion and to act like I knew everything was the strong, adult thing to do. I tried to underplay the importance of having someone to talk to, someone to hug, and someone supportive around me. I kept many of my thoughts and emotions to myself, thinking I could handle everything on my own. And in some ways teaching myself to hold back like that blocked me from being able to open up and share in important moments. I probably could've talked to my family about my problems, frustrations, and mistakes, but most times I was either too embarrassed about whatever I had done or scared I would get in trouble for it. As a child, I thought being an adult meant that you could do whatever you wanted to do and people just had to be okay with it. However, I've found adulthood to be more about crafting the discipline to do what's right regardless of what's convenient. But back then I didn't know any better. I was fine as long as I didn't let anyone see my worry, stress, and struggle. I didn't want pity. And I wasn't looking for my dad to suddenly take me in and be the dream father I always wanted him to be. I didn't need it.

People fear what they don't understand. I felt I knew nothing about my dad, and though I didn't fear him as a person, I feared trying to build a closer relationship with him. I felt a void as a result of the distance between us. I wasn't sure if I would ever let him close to me. Dana is not a bad person. There are things about him that I love. He was born in November, one of my favorite months. He's a Luther Vandross fan, which means he has good taste in music. He's a diehard Dallas Cowboys fan, and I've heard stories of how good he was when he played high school football. But you don't have to be a bad person for people to hate parts of their relationship with you. Growing up, there were parts of our relationship that I hated with a passion. I hated the way he never really spoke to my sister and me about anything interesting. If it wasn't quick comments about sports, work, or school, then his snoring filled the silence. My dad was proud of his work at the Newport News Naval Shipyard. He started right after high school and put in a lot of time. He loved it, but I hated the way he was always working overtime and we never did anything fun. I did not want to spend every other weekend, which is when we visited him, sitting around waiting for him to get off work. It never seemed to make a difference whether Elise and I were there or not. The whole arrangement felt forced as if he was only spending time with us because it was his turn and not because he wanted to be a father. I don't think Dana understood fatherhood beyond having a job, making weekend arrangements, and paying child support. Maybe it was never meeting his biological father that made him so passive about raising my sister and me. Anyway, to be living at his house then was an awkward situation. Perhaps if I could have spoken up, we'd become closer as a result, but if he didn't care enough to start the conversation, then I wasn't interested in having one.

————

When they were in grade school my parents, Dana and Monique, both lived in Camelot, a working-class neighborhood in Chesapeake, Virginia. They went to the same middle and high school. I'm hopeful that they were madly in love at some point, but from what I understand the foundation of their relationship was more based around familiarity. They were from the same place, going to school, and their houses were within five-minute walking distance of each other. My mom lived with her two sisters and both of her biological parents. My dad lived with his nine siblings, his mother, and the only father he knew, his stepdad. Dana and Monique's first child, my sister Elise, was born in 1985. I was born two years later. My parents were married for a few years in between but were divorced by my first birthday. To this day, it isn't often that one of them mentions the other unless a direct question is posed. They've kept the details of their story simple: "It didn't work out but we love our kids."

When Dana wasn't the topic of discussion, my mother wanted to talk to me about everything. We'd discuss everything from my problems with my friends to what happened at school to playing sports to girls. She loved talking to me about girls. Whether or not I actually opened up and told her what was on my mind, I always walked away from the conversation knowing a little more about Monique, how she saw the world, and who she was as a person completely separate from being my mom.

Let's go back in time to late May of 2005. The end of my senior year of high school.

For me, driving represented two things I felt I had neither of: control and the beginning of real freedom. The military doesn't ask the children of service members if they'd mind one more move. To defend our country service members need to have a mission-first mind-set. So for most of my life I got in my mother's car, my dad's car, or Uncle Sam's plane and went wherever the mission took us. I now wanted the freedom to determine my own destination. I just didn't want to start it off the way it did . . . with a sneaky car wreck, that is.

"Stay right there, I'm on the way," my mother said before she hung up the phone.

That was my first car accident behind the wheel. I was driving my girlfriend's car, which belonged to her parents. The mission was simple: drive five minutes from school to my house, pick some stuff up that I'd need for the gym, and do it all without getting caught by my mom. I had every move planned out, even parking two streets away so my mother would think I walked or got dropped off. I came in, made small talk, grabbed my gym bag, and walked back to the car. I felt good because my plan was working. I turned on the ignition and pulled out of the parking spot behind a passing truck.

Boom!

There was a low flatbed trailer hitched to the back of the truck. I didn't notice until it collided with the front driver's side of the car.

I was happy to be okay, but I knew I messed up. I knew how reckless this was.

And I knew there was only one person I could call.

My mom arrived in minutes. Other than being slightly winded from the walk, she was calm and completely in control of the situation. My mother explained to the driver of the truck that I was a minor without a license and should they call the police under these circumstances, I could be taken to jail. She told me to walk home, then she got behind the wheel of the car and waited with the truck driver until the police arrived. Then she, a fully licensed and insured driver, took responsibility for the accident. Her actions were swift. I could tell my mother wasn't questioning her decision. I was her son and I needed help. That was all that mattered to her.

I felt horrible for putting my mom in that position. Still, there was an even bigger part of me that believed this was an isolated incident, a fluke. I reasoned with myself that the trailer could've been hit by anyone at any time. I knew I was driving without a license, but I wasn't trying to hurt anyone, ya know? By the time I turned seventeen, I'd become comfortable with breaking rules that I didn't think mattered to me. My parents' rules, school rules, city/state laws, it didn't make a difference. I wanted what I wanted. While part of my mind-set at the time was adolescent naïveté, I was also comfortable taking my mother's love for granted. In fact, she covered for me so well that I didn't realize the depths of my trouble. My actions would have unintended consequences and I soon found out that there isn't always time to prepare and clean up before those consequences come.

Fast-forward to mid-June 2005.

High school graduation was a joyous time. Two days earlier I was recognized during an awards ceremony among my peers, the school faculty, and superintendents of the City of Chesapeake as Cooperative Career and Technical Education Student of the Year at Deep Creek High School. My parents threw an enormous cookout, inviting all of my friends and extended family to come eat, dance, drink, and celebrate my accomplishment. My parents were still upset about the accident, but they were also relieved I'd gotten my diploma and had been accepted to Norfolk State University. Graduating felt like I'd finally made them proud, a repayment for them giving me another chance. I was given $1,000 as a graduation gift from my family, but $700 of that went to pay for my parents' insurance deductible. I still came up $300 ahead.

As a show of good faith, my mother let me drive their Toyota Camry on graduation night to hang with my brother, Frankie, Frank's son. Frankie lived in Tennessee and I rarely got a chance to see him. With him in the car and having his license, and my permit in my wallet, I could legally drive. After pleading and reminding my parents of my skills, they agreed to let me drive down to the beach. Frankie would take us home. My close friend Joey, who also graduated, joined us for the festivities.

Frankie's graduation was a few weeks earlier in Tennessee. I wasn't able to attend but it felt good riding out with him that night. The air was full of possibilities and we were three high school graduates enjoying the night, fantasizing about how great our upcoming years of college would be. I felt invincible, like I could become anyone. Or at the very least, it felt like I was in for the best summer of my life. I was grown, or so I thought.

My diploma meant I was a man, capable of making my own decisions, steering my own ship. For now, though, I was driving my parents' car.

Two weeks later my mother hopped in the car with Frank to take my little sisters out for the afternoon, leaving me and their Dodge minivan at home alone. The plan: go visit Joey who lived only three miles away. I hadn't passed the driving test yet, which meant I still only had my permit. And there was no licensed driver at home to ride with me. So I grabbed the keys and took my chance.

Everything worked out fine last time, didn't it?

I am a risk-taker. You may be able to notice my tendency to be a bad one. I wasn't the kid who considered the consequences. Getting in trouble never worried me. My interest depended on my emotions, and my emotions changed on a whim. My desires were often limited and shortsighted, and having this immature perspective oftentimes made situations in my life more difficult than they needed to be.

"Wassup, Rob?" Joey greeted me like it was no big deal I'd just taken my parents' car to come over. Joey and a few other friends were in the middle of playing *Madden* so I sat down and got comfortable, which lasted all of fifteen minutes. Then Elise called, livid that I'd taken the car knowing I didn't have a license, and considering how it ended last time.

I didn't want the lecture.

She told me how irresponsible and selfish I was. I just wanted her to be quiet. To end the drama, I took the car home and was in my room, back in my basketball shorts, laughing at *Coming to America* by the time my parents returned with my little sisters. There was no way they would have known I'd even left the house.

Elise told on me.

The relationship between my older sister, Elise, and me is complicated, yet simple. In many ways she's my partner in discomfort, riding next to me when our dad, Dana, picked us up and dropped us off, and beside me in the middle seat as we flew back and forth across the world relocating from base to base. During those years Elise was the only person who knew what I was feeling. Only, we didn't actually talk to each other about what we felt. We fought a lot, arguing mostly over typical sibling stuff like toys, and then eventually attention. But at that point any argument we had was over my behavior. Elise is a lot like my mom. She's very loving, but also controlling. As the big sister, she exercised her authority over me. That was the last thing I wanted, another person feeling like they had a say over my life. So to teach me a lesson, Elise told.

My mother sat across from me in the living room with what had become an all too familiar look of disappointment. My stepfather, typically cooler about these matters, said nothing. Perhaps he was fed up with trying to soften my mother's firm words. Or perhaps he had no reason to continue to defend me. After all, it's not like I was really trying to defend myself.

"You refuse to learn from your mistakes, huh?" My mother's question didn't register at the time. I was too pissed. Pissed that

Elise ratted me out, pissed that I had to hear yet another lecture, pissed that all of that was for nothing because nothing bad actually happened. Frank was the patient one, simply offering, "You better get a clue." But my mom had had enough.

"Robert," she said. "I don't love you more than I love myself. You're costing me my peace and I can't have that. Either you get it together and live by our rules or you got to go."

As far as I was concerned, everyone was overreacting. I was grounded indefinitely. I couldn't go anywhere or do anything. The summer of promise, my last hurrah before I went to college, before adulthood took over, was going to be spent in the house with no cell phone, no television, and no friends. I couldn't even go to my family's Fourth of July barbecue. My punishment was to spend time alone and think about my actions. To think about how I was affecting others and what kind of person I wanted to be. And for what? All of this was because Elise wanted to prove a point? The whole thing felt stupid.

I'd just graduated weeks before, so to be on punishment, not permitted to see my friends, it all felt wrong. I, nonetheless, figured out a way to bend the rules. I'd wait until everyone left to make and receive all my phone calls. Elise was grown, and aside from being a detective the day she told on me, she had a life of her own and wasn't around often. My younger sisters were usually out with my mom, and Frank was working. Staying in touch with people wasn't as hard as it probably should've been.

As soon as my parents left the house for the family Independence Day barbecue, I called Joey. There was a DTLR Summer

Fest show at nTelos Pavilion (currently named Union Bank & Trust Pavilion) in Portsmouth, a concert I'd been looking forward to for months. I was forbidden to go because I was on lockdown. But here's the thing, no one was home. That's right. I repeat, no one was home.

I thought it was absurd that my parents thought they could still place me on punishment. My diploma meant I was grown enough to make decisions for myself. It was self-empowerment in the form of a piece of paper, stamped with the seal of approval from Deep Creek High School and the Virginia Board of Education. I'd earned the right to be regarded as an adult. So that evening Joey picked me up from my house and we went to see the show. But . . . the show was rained out after the opening acts and the headliner never showed. Then my mom called Joey's phone.

"I don't know where you're going to sleep tonight but you are not welcome to come back here. Goodbye!" my mother told me as I held the phone to my ear outside the concert.

I thought about the bag of clothes I'd packed and left at Joey's house. I knew that once I left—effectively breaking their rule—something bad was coming. Before I could hand him back his phone, it rang again. Unknown number, but I recognized the voice.

"Your mother says you can't come home." He paused. "I'm going to let you stay with me for a little bit, but just until you get a plan."

My dad Dana lived in Norfolk, Virginia, about a thirty-minute drive from our house in Chesapeake. After taking a week to adjust and think about my next move, my mom and Frank, along with Dana, made arrangements for me to move my things out of my parents' house. After I was done putting everything in the car, they asked me to talk for a moment.

"Sit down, son," my stepfather instructed.

Though we were the same height, as a military man, my stepfather carried a great presence. He didn't say much because he didn't need to. I'd used up all my passes as far as he was concerned. My mother, on the other hand, could make her five-foot, three-inch frame feel like she was seven feet tall when she became upset. And she was upset.

"We love you and we wish the best for you, but you've decided to live life in a way that we can no longer support."

I didn't know where my mother was going with this. I knew I'd messed up. I knew once again that I'd defied their wishes. But to say I was living life in a way that they couldn't support? There was no incident. No accident. No one was hurt. Why was this the tipping point? Why was this something we could not get over?

"Rob, when you're ready to grow up, we'll be here." Each one of my parents gave me a hug and I left with Dana. That was that. I was officially no longer welcome to live at my parents' house.

Since I couldn't go home, I convinced myself that home had no value. Could I have gotten back in the house? Probably. I considered writing a letter to my mother, explaining how I'd arrived at such a stupid decision. But I didn't. If I'd gone to my stepfather and spoken to him man-to-man, he might have talked to my mother on my behalf. But I didn't do that either. Both of those choices would've meant humbling myself enough to admit that I was wrong. And that was the last thing I wanted to do. Instead, I allowed myself to run free with desire. I was a man suddenly unburdened of responsibility to anyone but myself. I didn't have to answer to anyone and I could plan my days as I saw fit. My time was completely my own and I was free to spend it with whomever I pleased. As far as I was concerned, this was the beginning of adulthood and I was going to take full advantage.

I knew I needed to go hard in order to be on my own and ready to start college in the upcoming fall semester. My most immediate goals were to get a job, my license, and my own car. As a graduation gift, I was promised a 1995 four-door Ford Explorer from my grandfather, Frank's dad. But after it was decided that I would no longer be living there, they gave the truck to Elise.

Was I mad about that decision? Yes. Did I think it was petty of my parents to block a gift I earned by graduating? Yes. Could I do anything about it? No.

I had a place to stay thanks to Dana. Within two weeks I had a job selling cell phone accessories at kiosks in various malls. I was the guy sitting there all day long, answering questions about phone cases, chargers, antennas that light up, and reminding people that we didn't sell phone services, only phone accessories. The only real skill I needed was charm. I worked my smile and used my conversation skills to my advantage. I became a top company earner and gained the respect of the manager and kiosk owner quickly.

The next piece of my adult puzzle was to get my license. I enrolled in a three-week driving school. Sequoyah, my girl-friend at the time (well, she was my girlfriend in the sense that we agreed to break up before college, but we didn't just end things in one day), let me borrow her car to drive back and forth from driving school. Yes, after everything with my parents, I still drove Sequoyah's new car to driving school without a license every day for three weeks. I'd park around the corner so my in-structor and classmates wouldn't see me behind the wheel. I didn't really have a plan for what would happen if I got caught. I wanted my license and I knew that if I was careful I'd soon have it. The weeks breezed by and I was officially a licensed driver. Now that I had a job and my license, it was only a matter of time before I had a car.

To fill up my time, I began dating more. I searched for emo-tional support in relationships and I knew very little about set-ting healthy boundaries. I could tell when a woman liked me. I was always good about knowing that sort of thing. Growing up in a house with four women, I understood the subtle nuances and became adept at reading their body language.

I admired love but didn't value it very much. My approach to relationships with women was selfish simply because I wasn't looking to give anything. I wanted somebody to make me feel good about myself, and if they couldn't, I would find other ways to occupy my time. After my first few relationships in high school didn't go too well I became jaded. I was cheated on a few times. The most embarrassing time was watching my tenth grade girlfriend leave the movies with another guy. The entire basketball team watched as she walked out with her date, holding hands. Now, I'm not saying my experiences with ex-girlfriends is permission to be reckless with relationships. I knew using that as an excuse would be wrong. But, as a result of being hurt, I did start to guard my heart with Pentagon-level security. I preferred to carry a relationship status of single, but I wanted someone to spend consistent time with. I did not want anyone close enough to hurt, embarrass, or break me. While I made conscious efforts to shut myself off emotionally I didn't know that I could turn into a spiritual wreck while I was doing it. I thought I could brush anything off if given enough time. I mean who hasn't lied to themselves about their condition a time or two? We tell ourselves we're "okay" too often when we really are not.

Overall, I was happy that my current situation of living at Dana's meant that I was closer to being on my own. But I did not have peace in my life. It is hard to find peace or to find joy if you're not being honest with yourself. If I were, I would have admitted to being scared to death to start school, buy my own car, and eventually sign my name on a lease. I was scared to stop and let my family see me having regrets about my decisions. They wanted what was best for me in their mind but I was consumed with my own agenda. I'd become numb to their warnings because I decided they didn't really understand me. I didn't think they would ever forgive me. How could I ever earn back their trust?

"What is familiar is in danger of being taken for granted."
—Mark Nepo

Stubbornness and pride blurred my vision. My family was so familiar that I took them for granted. They were warning me to improve and slow down before making decisions because they loved me. My moves were motivated by pride, ego, and suppressed emotions—a mix that starts to make you live fast. What I mistook for nagging and judgment was actually my family showing me they cared; it was as if they were saying, "We notice an unhealthy pattern. Fix it before it really harms you." The truth is, when people love you, they tell you when you're wrong. When good people care about you, they push you to be responsible and expect you to be trustworthy.

Sometimes in our youth we aren't aware of the value of family. We appear as if we are happy and as if everything is going well. However, appearances ain't nothin'. I was hurting. Maybe I needed to be broken so that I could become the person I was meant to be. We would soon be able to tell.

Meanwhile, I took things one day at a time. My first semester as a college student was on the horizon and I wanted to start off strong. I missed my family. I missed hearing my mother's laugh, Frank's smoothies, and those daily hugs from my sisters. I missed it all, but I wasn't ready to go back. Not yet at least. I had some things I wanted to prove to myself first.

CHAPTER TWO

God Laughed at My Plan

September 2005, Labor Day weekend

I got my car!

I found out about the car from a guy working at the kiosk next to me in the mall. They sold electronics and he randomly mentioned that it was time to sell his old car. The asking price was $2,500. Dana and I drove to Hampton to check the car out the next night. The pearl-blue 1992 Honda Accord had 100,000 miles on it. The back windows didn't work, though everything else was in solid shape. Dana checked under the hood, crawled under the car, and inspected every tire. I wondered how he had so much experience with this, then I remembered how many different cars he drove when we were younger.

I'd saved up some money, but barely a quarter of what I needed to purchase the car. Dana suggested I ask Frank and my mom to help out. I didn't even know how to have that conversation with them. But my desire to own a car pushed me outside of my comfort zone. I talked with my parents and we worked out a deal. My mom would take out a loan and I would pay them back monthly. Two days later it was official. No more borrowing other people's cars or waiting for a ride. I was mobile and ready to go. Having a car supported my I-refuse-to-sit-still lifestyle. If there was a promise of action somewhere other than where I was, then that's where I had to go. It wasn't fresh off the lot or the latest model, but it was mine. This car would get me back and forth between school, work, my friends' houses or wherever else I wanted to go.

By this point I was two weeks into my freshman year at Norfolk State University.

Behold the Green and Gold!

NSU is a fully accredited, Division 1 HBCU (Historically Black College or University). Because I would not be living on campus, my tuition was under $11,000. I filled out the Free Application for Federal Student Aid (FAFSA) and received a Pell Grant to cover my academic year. I enrolled in the School of Business, with entrepreneurship as my major. I intended to do well in college, though in high school I considered myself an okay student. Then I focused more on sports and social life than I did on academics. I graduated with a 2.8 GPA. My approach to NSU was just like all of the other schools I visited over the years; it was just another place to get used to. I'd be there for four years. I didn't have to worry about being uprooted and shipped off to another school in the middle of the year. I could get comfortable, settle in, and enjoy college.

On my first day of classes, I remember wanting to call my mom to talk me out of being nervous. No matter where we were in the world, she always made the first day of any school year feel special. I never expressed to my mom how important it was to make her proud of me. I listened every time she and her circle of friends talked about the value of college. Though my mom never went to college, she believed it was the key to a successful future. "Nowadays they won't even look at your résumé unless you have a bachelor's, soon it will be a master's." Well, I considered myself a smart person and I wanted a successful future, so college would be my time to show and prove, an opportunity to make sure my parents knew I was capable of doing big things. But I knew it all would be an uphill battle. My mother was skeptical as well. I knew this because NSU wasn't even my first choice. I actually wanted to go to Hampton.

I got accepted to Hampton.

Hampton University is a private HBCU and at a little over $35,000 a year for tuition with room and board. To go to Hampton is not cheap at all. I wasn't concerned with the cost though. I wanted to go to Hampton because the campus vibe was electric, the students walked with a pride I didn't see often. Elise was already a junior on campus and my aunt Shelia Hillman (my dad Dana's sister) is an alumnus. She was a three-time all-American in basketball. I liked the idea of being on the same campus with

Elise, joining the tradition—granted that there was enough distance to not drive each other crazy. Nonetheless, I'd heard and seen enough. I wanted in.

My mother had other plans for me. On the one hand, she always spoke highly of me to her friends and colleagues. She held high hopes for my future and told me I was a natural-born leader. On the other hand, she would openly and often doubt my ability to make the right decisions.

When the Hampton acceptance letter arrived, she quickly told me to forget it. First reason: too expensive. I thought we could figure out how to pay for it the same way it happened for Elise. The second reason was a bit more complicated. My mother didn't think I'd take college serious enough to justify paying my tuition at Hampton. For her, a state public school like NSU where I could get an education that was completely covered through my financial aid was more practical. I understood her thought process. Free school does sound better than paying for courses. But I was accepted to Hampton on my first try. I qualified. I was just hoping she would be happy for me. I wanted some points for that.

None were coming. That conversation was a done deal the moment she said, "Forget it." I struggled to let go of how hurtful it was to hear her being so candid, doubting my ability and commitment to my future. I was certain that if she was the student shuffling from school to school, then she would have more compassion for my inconsistent academic motivation.

Nevertheless, college was upon me. All of that was behind us.

Freshman week made NSU feel like the campus that never slept. There was something going on every single night—dorm parties, game nights, date auctions, frat parties, you name it. I chose to see and experience as much as I could. I enjoyed NSU for the same reason I did every new school. I loved the girls. Norfolk had a lot of girls. Sure, the school had academic offerings, the football and basketball programs, Greek life, and there were some legendary soul food spots near campus. But what excited me the most was the beauty, confidence, and style of the ladies. Short ones, tall ones, thick, slim, light, dark, all hues. Suddenly I was seated at a buffet of the opposite sex and I was hungry.

When it came to choosing classes for my curriculum I was also hungry. After all the drama of the summer I just wanted to coast through the first semester. I wanted classes where I could get easy As. Most of my classes were introductory courses: freshman orientation, English 101, Psychology 101, college mathematics, and health. I didn't even pretend to be interested in those courses. I'd sit in class watching the clock, awaiting my chance to go do something else.

The plan to pass the semester was manageable: I'd follow the syllabus and do a little work every day, enough to complete the assignments, receive credit, and do decent on tests and exams. It was the same plan I used in high school. It worked for me then. That 2.8 GPA was enough to get me into NSU and I figured my same approach would be enough to keep me there. The work would get done somehow.

And it did, sometimes late and other times with only half of my attention. I did just enough not to fail. I passed every class. I was selected as Mr. Freshman for Homecoming. Things seemed to be going well. College life wasn't perfect, but I was making it work.

I had a 2.7 GPA when my first semester ended and I was proud. My mother was not. "A 2.7? I think you can do better than a 2.7, Robert."

Maybe I could. I knew it was possible for me to study more, work harder on assignments, and pay more attention to lectures. But I didn't want to fight about it.

"Ma, I'm doing the best I can."

"Stay focused. You can get better," was all she said.

That New Year's Eve I went to church with my mother, Frank, and my sisters.

The year 2006 started off fast.

First, I lost my job selling cell phone accessories.

The holiday season wasn't as big as expected. The owner was downsizing the company to one kiosk and didn't need as many employees. So I got a job working in E & E's barbershop through a connection from a family friend. I wasn't a licensed barber, but I was very good at cutting hair. It was a skill I'd learned while we were traveling throughout my childhood. I was very particular about my appearance and the way my hair looked. I loved having soft curly hair and when I wore it low, I always received compliments on my waves. I considered hair a big part of my physical identity, so it was exhausting trying out new barbers, city to city, only to be disappointed when I left with a jacked-up hairline. I took things into my own hands when I got my first pair of clippers in the seventh grade. I needed to know how to do my own edge-up before I was forced to learn how to ask for one in German. Besides mowing lawns, cutting hair was my first hustle.

I enjoyed working in the barbershop for many reasons. It was a dream of mine to be the go-to barber. I imagined some kid like me walking into a shop for the first time, nervous about the way he would look walking out. He would look over and see me working, nod and ask to be next. I made sure every haircut was sharp. I wanted the experience to feel like a personal transformation. Like one of those *Ricki Lake* makeovers I would see on TV. Most of my clients were people from Camelot and my old high school Deep Creek. I think they trusted me because they liked the waves in my hair. I would always get the question "Who cut your hair?" and I loved to proudly respond, "Me!" I was my own personal billboard for new clients. And something magical happened when they would sit in my chair. As I prepped my clippers and lay the cape over their chest to catch the falling hair, I would see a subtle moment of release. The feeling that said, "I'm trusting you, bro. I know you got me."

When someone was in my chair, it was like I instantly became a therapist. My clientele was mostly black men and when you're a good barber they will talk to you about anything—stress on the job, discord in the family, current events, or just general opinions on how to view life. Of course, there are conversations on topics like sports, politics, and who was acting a fool at the club the night before. But it's all love, it's fellowship, and it's authentic. If you have no idea what I'm saying right now, go to your Internet browser and type in the words "Ice Cube Barbershop," then watch the first two movies. I cannot vouch for the third. To put it plainly, in the shop I had stature, my thoughts were respected, my work was valued and appreciated. It was my first time feeling all of these things in one place.

As my second semester at NSU approached, I planned to better apply myself. Surely, it'd be easier to buckle down now. All I had to do was stay focused on school, the barbershop, and away from trouble.

I've heard that the best way to make God laugh is to tell him you have a plan. I think I was slowly becoming his favorite co-median. I realized quickly that no matter how focused you are on a plan, things don't always happen the way you want them to.

First, my car failed inspection.

It was February and I needed new brakes. If I didn't get the money soon, I would be parking it and needing a ride again. Turns out a $2,500 car will usually only give you $2,500 worth of miles and I was pushing it around Virginia like it was brand-new, off the lot. Though I was doing well in the barbershop, I wasn't saving any money. The cash was gone almost as soon as it came in.

Then, in March, Teo died.

Let's go back in time a bit.

"Your father's outside!" My mother's announcement sig-naled the beginning of the same adventure every other week-end.

It was time for Elise and me to spend the weekend with our dad Dana. On Friday the first stop was usually to see some family. An uncle, one of our aunts, or we'd go to Camelot to see our Grandma Ida. We'd have dinner and then go to his house for a night of TV. Saturday mornings were different. My father worked overtime at the shipyard every weekend, even when he had us. Sometimes we would stay at his house with our uncle Robin, but if given a choice we always asked to go over to Aunt Sharon's house. She is Teo's mom.

Now, Sharon isn't a blood relative. But she, no less, is my aunt. I'll explain. My grandparents Papa and GeGe started in Kansas before Papa joined the navy, they then moved to California and Japan before settling in Virginia with my mom and her sisters. Their three daughters in order of oldest to youngest are Daiquiri, Monique (my mom), and Derricka. Papa was a chief petty officer in the navy, GeGe was a manager at a factory that made apparel. In retirement they made Virginia their home and built an extended family there. My grandparents often spent time at a social club called the American Legion, and there they met Aunt Sharon's parents. Her mom, Ruby, became a best friend to my GeGe. When it was time to go over to each other's house for a cookout, Sunday football, or a Friday night party, all the kids would play together. Aunt Sharon is older than my mom and her sisters, so she became "big sis" in a way. When they all had kids around the same time, the cycle happened again. Teo had all sisters and girl cousins. I had all sisters and girl cousins. We were the boys and we were close.

Thaddius Orlando Weston Jr. was my first friend, the first person I identified as a brother. From sunup to sundown, every other Saturday, Elise and I went from being a pair to being a part of a squad. Sharon's two daughters, Angie and Erica, were sister-friends to GeGe's grandkids Elise and my aunt Daiquiri's daughters Tori and Jewell. Everything Elise couldn't say to me she could ramble on with them about for hours. They did what I knew girls did for fun: talk about boys, make dance routines, hair, nails, play dress up, act out roles from *House Party*, watch shows like *Martin* and *The Fresh Prince of Bel Air*. It was cool to be around them, but Teo and I liked our time separate when we could manage to find some.

Teo had a relationship with his father, Thad, that was similar to my relationship with Dana. We bonded over the fact that we only saw our fathers on occasion. However, I was thankful whenever "time with my dad" converted into a good Saturday with my bro. Teo was a year older, almost a foot taller, and had this natural cool about him that felt like it couldn't be real coming from a kid. But it was real. He was real. And I always wanted to impress my big brother. I wanted to show him I was cool too. If Teo threw the football, then I told myself I had to make a sweet catch and throw back a better spiral. If we raced, though I knew he was faster, I always made sure I was the one saying "On your mark . . . Get set . . . Go!" I knew I couldn't beat him, but if I was the one saying "Go," then I could get at least get the first step in the race. He made me laugh, like that "my cheeks and stomach are starting to hurt" kind of laugh. On sleepovers I'd ask him, "You sleep?" and he had the same reply every time, "Nah, I'm just resting my eyes." Teo was my best friend before I realized what a best friend really was. And it stayed that way even after my mother married Frank and we began to move. I always carried a piece of Teo with me.

"You ever kissed a girl?" Teo asked me one day while we threw the football back and forth.

I already knew about Teo and the ladies. All the girls loved him. Meanwhile I was still figuring out how to pull off holding a girl's hand.

"Not yet, but I plan to," I said, throwing a perfect spiral back. Teo just smiled.

In 2006, toward the end of February, Teo called me and told me he got baptized. He'd spent the first three weeks of the month in jail and didn't want to go into detail about it. I was all about school, barbershop, and staying out of trouble at the time. Since I was so busy we hadn't really talked much. During our last conversation he was in Richmond at Job Corps, a free residential education and job training program. On that call, he told me God had spoken to him. The message was that he needed to turn his life around and spend more time around me in order to fly straight. I wasn't sure how he saw me in a position to help him do that, but if he said "God said it" then *God said it*. I told him he needed to enroll with me at NSU. I reminded him of how our grandparents would bring us out to the tailgate on campus before football games when we were younger.

"Man, I don't know how to get into college. I'm getting a job somewhere," Teo responded. I told him to give me some time to change his mind.

On the afternoon of March 2, I left NSU's campus on the way to the barbershop to cut hair when Teo called my cell phone. He was home getting ready for work. It was his first week working warehouse at the Wal-Mart in Chesapeake, near my parents' house.

"It's a start," he said. I could tell in his tone that he wasn't impressed with himself.

I responded, "Damn right it is. We celebrating your new start this weekend too. I want you to come to the Legion with me."

"Man, this girl told me about that. It's the Saturday night jank in Hampton, right, twelve to four a.m.?" I could hear Teo smiling as he described the party.

"I thought you said college life wasn't for you? How you know about everything?" I shot back.

"If there's beautiful women dancing in a party every week, you know I'm going to find out about it. I hope they play reggae and Cash Money all night. I'm off work this weekend too. We in there!" Teo had a way of making his excitement contagious.

"Yo, I'll hit you back when I get home after work. My ride is here," Teo said.

"Aight, bro. Later."

We hung up.

Teo got a ride to work that day from Thad. In hindsight, I don't know that I'd ever heard Teo say, "My dad is coming to get me," and I'm not sure how I would've reacted if he had.

"My ride is here."

That was it.

Elise called first. It had been an hour since my conversation with Teo, and I was in the middle of a haircut. I could hear the fear in her voice as soon as I answered. "Rob, something happened."

She told me that Teo was in the passenger seat of Thad's Nissan Maxima riding down Interstate 64 when Thad turned off the exit close to Battlefield Blvd. Police estimate he must have been driving close to seventy miles per hour when he took the sharp turn.

Thad was killed instantly.

My mother beeped in while I was on the call with Elise.

"Rob, I need you to come to the hospital. This might be the last time you get to speak to Teo."

The elevator door opened and I walked out into the arms of my mother. She pulled me to the side.

"Robert, I love you so much. Now, Teo is not going to look the way you remember him. I'm just warning you now before you walk into the room. I need you to be strong."

I didn't know what to tell myself, much less her. She and Aunt Sharon had known each other for a very long time. My mom watched Teo grow up and loved him like another son. Her eyes were glossy and I could tell she had been crying.

When I walked into the room I felt my knees buckle a bit. There he was, just lying there. The skin on the top of his head was the deepest, most beautiful lavender I'd ever seen. His eyes were swollen shut. There were tubes coming out of places in his scalp where his dreads once were. It reminded me of the time I gave him a bald spot at my aunt Daiquiri's house. I was playing with a pair of her husband's clippers and called myself giving him an edge-up. We were young, no more than eleven or twelve, and I had no idea what I was doing. I was just imitating our barber. He sneezed and I didn't move the clippers fast enough. When he looked and saw the fresh bald spot on his scalp reflected in the mirror, he took off running out of the house. He didn't want anyone to see his hair all messed up and I was sure we would get in trouble for using the clippers without permission. I was caught somewhere between the humor of how fast he took off and fear that I'd need faster hands when he came back ready to fight.

But this day we wouldn't be fighting. Or even talking. And he wouldn't be running after seeing this bald spot. He was in a condition that I never imagined seeing. I didn't want to lose my brother. Dying at nineteen years old was too soon. His mom said pray, my mom said pray, everybody in the room was praying. I grabbed his forearm, looking directly into his face. I was not praying. In my heart I was saying goodbye because I knew my brother wasn't responding.

The next morning at seven my mother called from the hospital. I was at my dad Dana's house. She told me that Teo was pronounced brain-dead and his family made the decision to remove him from life support.

For the next few days I was angry, sad, confused, and bewildered. Young people just die like that? Good ones? Is this really the world we're living in? My best friend was gone and I did not understand how it all happened so quick. We were just talking. I did not want to accept that there would be no more conversations. No more moments. I thought about being angry at his father for driving so fast on an exit ramp, but he was gone too.

I wanted a hug from my dad Dana. A good one, just like the one I gave him outside of the church when his mom, my grandmother Ida, passed away. My mom, Elise, and I flew from Germany to Virginia to be at her funeral. But in the five days between Teo's death and his funeral, I didn't get a hug from Dana once. I knew he could hear me sobbing in my rented room, less than thirty feet away from him. He knew how close Teo and I were. He'd helped create that bond. He'd relied on it every other Saturday when he was working. And now the pinch hitter was dead. Teo departed a great son and my hero. As for Dana, any patience I had to further develop our relationship went to zero.

After that day, I never went back to his house.

I drove to the church for the funeral alone. My only stop was the barbershop to give myself an edge-up. I pulled up and parked with everything I owned piled between the trunk and the back seat.

The ceremony was a family affair. I was sad that this was the reason we were all together in harmony, but also grateful. Sometimes it takes an ugly unexpected loss to remind you of all that you have in life. Family, friends, time to breathe and try things again—it is all a gift.

By the middle of April, I stopped going to most of my classes. I was burdened by many questions about life and so much inner turmoil. I felt lost. Life wasn't panning out the way it was supposed to.

The school year didn't end well. I finished the semester on autopilot with my GPA dropping with the speed of elevators in a high-rise building. Teo's death affected me in a way I did not expect. It made me want to be alone. Generally, I couldn't concentrate, especially when it came to school. Classes felt longer than they were. Sitting still was exhausting. I thought about Teo so much. I wanted to call him to tell him how much I was thinking about him. I'd sit in class wondering, *What am I doing here?* At first I hyped myself up by saying I was in college to live out both of our dreams. But I didn't have the motivation to do anything. And though I chose to stop going back to my dad's house, part of me was raging and disappointed that he never came looking for me.

After final grades posted, I only passed one class, physics. I got a B, which I counted as a victory because I'd gotten a D in high school physics.

I failed English 102 due to absences.

Summer 2006

After an argument with the shop owner, I stopped cutting hair. I still didn't have my license, nor did I have any logging of official hours, so going to another barbershop seemed pointless. I decided to make house calls instead.

In July, Papa began intensive treatments to fight lymphatic cancer. I was always close with my grandparents, although I didn't see them as often as I wanted to. Papa let me move in with them to help watch the house. They spent most of the summer staying three and a half hours away at The University of North Carolina at Chapel Hill, where my Papa started receiving chemotherapy. So besides a few family visits, I had the house to myself. I took full advantage of the opportunity and would often invite company over, way more than I ever would have if my grandparents were home.

"*Dying inside but outside you're looking fearless*": Tupac said it best. That was me. Fronting like I was on top of everything. Yet I was still coping with the death of my best friend and facing a growing dissatisfaction with myself. I wanted to stay busy. I got a new job at Target. My friend Miran and I started out on the night shift unloading trucks from three a.m. to twelve thirty in the afternoon. It was mindless work. Pick up a box, move it somewhere else, put the contents on the shelf. At least being alongside Miran made it fun. We cracked jokes all night.

After a few weeks I was promoted to "shoe specialist" and given my own section selling affordable footwear. Having my own department to look after felt like an accomplishment. I was solid as a salesman. I could see what someone was thinking by the way they walked, the words they used, what they weren't saying, their body language. My ability to assess customers earned me a lot of respect with my supervisors. I was also given a walkie-talkie. Soon enough I was attending manager meetings. It wasn't exactly the career path I saw for myself but for the moment it wasn't so bad.

Fall 2006

I decided going back to school was the best option for me.

I started the fall on academic probation. My mom helped me write a letter to the dean of admissions asking for a second chance. I made the same promises to myself that I hoped to keep the year before. *I'll work harder. I'll stay focused. No more partying. I'll lay off all the time devoted to girls.* I was going to prove to everyone that I deserved another shot.

That September, Miran and I decided to take a trip to New Jersey for my nineteenth birthday to meet up with some friends that I knew from when I lived there. Target did not approve my days off, so I quit, just walked out after my shift on the last day of work before my trip. I convinced my cousin Danielle to rent a car for us. We were too young to rent and I didn't trust my old Honda to make the trip. I drove behind her to the Enterprise car rental out by the airport, handed her $150 cash and watched as she drove off the lot with a black Buick LaCrosse. Was it illegal? Sure. But what could go wrong? We'd only be gone for two days. We hit the road early with the MapQuest directions printed out. Those were the days before phones had built-in GPS apps.

Miran and I were on our way, cruising on the Chesapeake Bay Bridge, listening to Jay-Z's *Unplugged* version of "Song Cry" featuring Jaguar Wright. It's an all-time favorite of mine. I was excited to get away. Compared to the Accord, the Buick was a major upgrade. Much smoother, faster, I could barely feel bumps on the road. My plan was to stay at seventy miles per hour. The speed limit was fifty-five but seventy put us just ahead of the flow of traffic. Then I saw flashing blue lights in the rear-view mirror.

According to Officer Pike, I was driving ninety-eight miles per hour in a fifty-five-mile-per-hour zone. Before asking Miran and me to step out of the vehicle, he asked if we had any weapons on us. Of course, we both said we didn't. Once I was out of the car, the officer frisked me. Then matters quickly got intense as he threw me down on the asphalt pavement. He was yelling at me, "What's this, son?" I had totally forgotten that I had a box cutter on me from work. In my mind, a box cutter wasn't a weapon, it was just something that made my job easier. The officer thought otherwise. He asked us about the car and since I couldn't prove I had permission to drive it on the rental agreement, he impounded it and placed Miran and me in the back seat of his car. He drove a little ways on the bridge until he could turn around and take us to a station on the southbound side. Instead of locking us up, he gave me a ticket for reckless driving, explained that the court date in November was mandatory, then said we were free to go. So here we were still on the Chesapeake Bay Bridge, which is seventeen miles long. I asked him to take us to the end of the bridge so we could at least get picked up without someone having to pay the twelve-dollar toll both ways. He refused and told us our options: "You can either start walking or come sit in this cell until we find somewhere else to put you."

We walked to The Thimble Shoal Island Visitors Center and stayed there until seven p.m. We had no clue who would pick us up and I refused to call my mom. Not to mention our cell phones were dying by then. Finally, a nice black family came by the rest stop. We explained what happened, and they were kind enough to give us a ride to Norfolk. From there Miran had a friend pick us up and take us to my grandparents' house in Chesapeake where our cars were. As soon as we arrived, we jumped into Miran's car, which was in need of a new tire, and got back on the road to New Jersey.

The trip was great. I came back ready to focus on improving my GPA.

Young and dumb, I wasn't fazed by the ticket. I'd deal with it later. I threw it in a drawer with the rest of the citations I'd been collecting.

November 2006

"You're just not going to learn, are you, son?"

That's what the Virginia Beach county judge said just before sentencing me to serve eighty days for reckless driving and failure to pay three speeding violations. My heart sunk as I stood there in the courtroom. *Eighty days!*

"Judge, wait a minute! I have a job and I'm a college student . . . I can't go to jail!"

Those were my exact words as the bailiff instructed me to put both of my arms behind my back. When he turned to cuff me, that's when I saw Officer Pike with a look of satisfaction on his face. Why did this make him so happy? He looked like a Nascar guy who could appreciate a "pedal to the metal" attitude. I was used to driving a slow old hooptie with a four-cylinder engine, but the Buick was an elegant chariot that had six. I just wanted to test the gears out. Guess I picked the wrong bridge on the wrong day.

"They won't let me out, they won't let me out (I'm locked up)." Akon's hit anthem suddenly had new meaning as it played on repeat in my head.

Virginia Beach City Jail was my new home for the next eighty days. Getting booked was horrible: stripping down naked, being searched, coughing, bending, and then having your picture taken after it all. Feeling violated is an understatement. Just as I hoped to never see the mug shot photo, it was printed on the band they attached to my wrist. My cell looked the way you might imagine it would. There was a bunk bed, a steel toilet with a mini sink attached to it, and a cell door. I was given a blanket, toothbrush, a miniature bar of soap, a pillowcase, and a whole lot of time to think.

"You don't belong here. Nobody expects you to be here," I told myself this over and over.

That first night, I sat in the cell thinking about my dad Dana. I'd gone to that same jail to visit him during my senior year of high school. He was there serving 180 days for multiple DUIs, five to be exact. I remember feeling shame as I looked at my father from behind the Plexiglas barrier. *How could you let yourself get here?* I thought. Only then, as I lay in my cell, staring at the steel door, I felt like I was sitting in his same seat. I felt embarrassed. I thought of questions about how his time locked up affected him.

Did he work out?
Did he write?
Were there any arguments or fights with cellmates?
Did he dream?
Did he think about me?

When I learned Dana had legal troubles, I wasn't the friend and support a son should be. I was more concerned with enjoying my last year of high school than anything else. Basketball season and school were my only concerns. He would call and check in on me from the jail when he saw my basketball stats in the newspaper, but after a few minutes of small talk, I didn't have much to talk about and besides, AT&T would let us both know that he was running out of minutes. I thought it was cool that he kept up with our team even though he couldn't be there for the actual games. Part of me resented the desire I had for him to see me play varsity basketball in person. It was one of the reasons I was excited to move back to Virginia for my last year. I imagined myself having a big game and him watching proudly from the stands. Then I would snap back to reality because another part of me knew there was nothing he could do about it.

Here I was, nineteen years old, failing out of college, sentenced to eighty days, and freezing in my orange jumpsuit because it's cold in jail in November.

Jails can be extremely overpopulated. Though the cells are built for two inmates, there are creative ways to add more if necessary. I had two cellmates. One who slept above me and another who slept on the floor adjacent to my rack. On my second day, after talking to my cellmate who slept on the floor, I learned that I would only be required to serve 10 percent of my eighty-day sentence. This meant that I could make bail after day eight. Hearing that news, I finally worked up the courage to call my mother. My whole life she'd told me that if I went to jail, she would not visit me or get me out. When I called her I wasn't expecting much. I just wanted to let her know that I'd be away for a few days and not to worry if she hadn't heard from me. The phone rang seven times, my heart sinking farther and farther into my stomach with each ring. I got the answering machine and quickly hung up. I couldn't drop the news to her as a voice mail. What if my little sisters heard it? To them I was a super-hero. I could do no wrong.

I called my aunt Daiquiri, who I knew worked with teens in group homes. I knew she would not judge me. She answered the phone, but as soon as she said hello the operator took over. "You have a collect call from _____, an inmate in the Virginia Beach City Jail. Do you wish to accept this call?" When you call, there is a pause by the operator so that the inmate can say their name. I'd never been more ashamed to say "Robert Hillman" in my life. Even if I wasn't proud of all the decisions I'd made, I'd always been proud to say my name. She accepted the call.

Her first words were "Are you okay?" It felt good to hear her voice. I assured her I was fine but I could hear the concern in her tone. Our conversation was relatively casual despite the situation. I asked her to pass the information along to my mother and to let everybody know that I was okay. She said she would handle it, told me that she loved me, and then the call ended.

That was rock bottom. I felt broken.

The third day, my family visited. Frank, my mom, and Elise. I was ashamed that they had to see me in that dingy jumpsuit and handcuffs. We talked, they watched as I ate dinner, and my mom promised she would be back the next day. It was hard to pick my head up and look at them the entire conversation. I started to think about how other members of my family would react. What would my friends say? I genuinely thought I was a good person despite my flaws, mistakes, insecurities, and bad decisions. But Rob the inmate contradicted all of that. We are judged by our actions, not by our intentions. Where did this "I can make a million bad decisions but I'm still a good guy because I mean well" attitude come from?

That night I asked myself some serious questions:

Who am I?
What type of person do I want to be?
Do I want to be the reason my family is ashamed?
Am I a failure?
Will my mother ever respect me again?
Why does God have me here right now?

I couldn't sleep. I was scared to be in jail, but even worse, I was scared to get out of jail with no direction. There was a hole burning inside of me. It felt like a piece of me was missing. I lacked purpose. I didn't know where I wanted to go or who I wanted to be.

On the eighth night, at ten p.m., my mother bailed me out.

I was happy to be a free man, but I knew I was a long way from being the kind of person who would never end up there again. To be that person would require something more of me, something far greater than I had ever given.

I was embarrassed. I didn't even talk to my mom after she bailed me out. I tried to catch up on my assignments from school but I missed important notes and instructions. I ignored her phone calls. I wouldn't go to her house and I barely stayed at the same place two nights in a row. I remember thinking going to the recreation center to play basketball would help get things off my mind. As soon as I walked in, guys were joking on me for being locked up for a traffic offense. They imitated a buff guy with a small voice being in a jailhouse encounter. "What you in for, big dawg?" one asked the other. After puffing up his chest he responded in a high-pitched voice, "Parking tickets!" The whole gym erupted in laughter. For them, being locked up for traffic offenses was soft. I played through the jokes, knowing that that kind of thing just came with the territory in Camelot. I'd seen other people get ripped worse for doing simple things like missing a layup. Leaving the gym, I had two missed calls from my mom, which I didn't return. That night I slept over at my friend Corey's house.

At seven a.m. my mother knocked on the door.

"I don't care what you've done," she said standing at the screen door. "No matter what's going on in your life, don't ever hide from me." I just stood there. My mom never asked why I ignored her or what was happening. It didn't matter. She just needed to lay her eyes on me, to see for herself that I was okay. "Don't ever hide from me." That was all she needed to say. There was something in the way she said it, the relief in her voice, the way it felt as much like a request as it was an order. Those five words felt like a bond between us. And in them she was giving me a valuable life lesson: You never put your personal issues before your relationship with your family, especially your mother.

Dear Mama,

I had a habit of messing up. I was a liar, a user, and flat out selfish.
I tested you, pushed you, and ran from you.
Yet you loved me when I least deserved it.
In spite of it all your heart refused to quit on me.

You weren't intimidated by odds or statistics, you knew what you were up against in raising me but you fought anyway.
You didn't just preach unconditional love, your actions showed it.
You were the first person to support me in anything.
In the midst of my fears you assured me I could face it all.
If I ran, you would run to me. If I pushed you would pull me closer.
You made sure I knew I was valuable to you.
You promised to always be there, and you have always kept your promises.

You taught me the importance of family, love, and relationships.
You showed me that real men take care of home, they never run from it.
You taught me the value of my word and my name, and you held me accountable for my actions.
You never let life take your smile.

Mom, I adore everything about you.

Your compassion, your selflessness, your faith.
Your warmth, your strength, your patience.
Your spirit, your love, your life.

I thought moving out of my parents' house meant that the closeness between my mom and me was gone. But in a way, being locked up put me in a position to see just how much I needed her in my life. The situation brought us closer.

> We are all just one choice away from a completely different life.

I realized I was not as in control of my life as I thought I was. I had two choices: I could tell myself that I had nothing to look forward to and remain the person with high hopes and little results. Or I could face reality, stop trying to make excuses for my bad decisions, and work to become a better person.

I chose the latter.

CHAPTER THREE

Time to Sacrifice

Spring 2007

Social media was growing faster and faster. Everybody on campus was on Facebook. I'd walk into the library's computer lab and see all of the screens showing the same website. Facebook has grown to become a platform to connect people, businesses, and cultures in countries across the globe. But it started as a place for college students to meet other college students online. And in its first few years, to access Facebook, you needed an ".edu" suffix at the end of your email. Only, I didn't have my own computer so my time exploring was limited. But every chance I got, I checked Facebook and I saw how addicting it could be scrolling, clicking, having conversations with people I'd yet to see or speak with in person.

Facebook was a new kind of online experience. Before, going

onto the Internet for me meant AOL browsers, Yahoo, and slow dial-up connections that blocked important phone calls from coming through.

At sixteen, I remember sharing my first poem online as my AIM (AOL Instant Messenger) away message. On AIM, the away status was a marker you put on your account to show that you are unavailable at the moment. The message was whatever you wanted people to see while you were away. I chose a short original poem I'd written. And when I returned to AIM, there were messages saying that the poem was beautiful, or relatable, and there were questions asking, "Who wrote it?" I purposely didn't put my name after the poem. Though I wanted feedback and approval, I was more worried about the blows of rejection that could come if people hated it. Thankfully, that wasn't the response I received at all. The reactions were more like, "I love this and I want to read more. Direct me to the author." From there I wanted to begin letting the world know I was a talented writer. And I knew the online community would help me do it.

Writing is something I began doing after my mom married Frank. We came together to form a beautiful family, but when we traveled for the military, I found it difficult to be away from my grandparents, cousins, and aunts in Virginia. They were my sounding board. In Virginia, if I didn't remember a story or the name of something, I was usually around someone who did. I could easily turn to my cousin and ask, "Hey, remember when we were six and went to Busch Gardens . . ." They would know the exact trip I was talking about, making the memory something we shared. But when we moved from place to place, I'd always have to make new memories with new people.

When I'd attend a new school, there was no reminiscing among friends. If a group of kids started talking about elementary school, rec league sports games, or the first dance they all attended together I would just sit and listen like I knew the story too. I tried to find pockets within the story where I could share something about myself, but generally, talking about the past felt like a waste. I started thinking of my stories as the type that were meant to be told later, when I could connect the separated dots of my life into one clear picture.

When I traveled away from Virginia, I started journaling. I just wrote my thoughts down on the page, whatever came to mind. I wrote about the way my relationships with my two dads made me feel. I journaled about the couples I observed at school. Every day some guy and a girl argued about who wasn't doing something right in the relationship. It was hilarious to see my classmates talk about being together forever. *Yeah right, a few miles would break y'all up in a week,* I thought to myself. My more optimistic journal entries came when I was writing about my goals and dreams for life. I wasn't trying to be a writer, I just liked having a place to release my feelings.

At times, I am able to say on the page what I don't know how to say to the people around me. The page is patient and forgiving, so I go there first with any emotional problems I may have. Writing is how I learned to articulate my thoughts, recognize my voice, and to validate myself. When I'm looking for someplace to unload and vent, I can say what I want and express myself fully in my journal. Nobody grades it or offers an unnecessary critique, or anything like that. The page just waits until I return ready to speak again.

At the start of the semester, I enrolled in Writing Poetry II as an elective. I chose it mainly because of my passion for writing, but more to see who else was writing around me. Out of the other classes on my schedule, this was the one that had me excited for the first day. I got there early, needing a good spot in the room. Anytime I was seated in the back or against a wall in a classroom it was harder for me to stay focused. I preferred to be in a center seat toward the front. As students rolled in, some alone and others in groups, I quickly noticed that the class was filled with upperclassmen. I felt young. The last thing I wanted was for someone to look at me and think, *What is he doing here?*

The professor asked us to call him by his first name, Daniel, which right away made me like him. I took it as a sign that he wanted to establish a more personal vibe than the traditional professor-student relationship. He was white, late twenties, and looked more like a graduate student than a teacher. But what impressed me the most was his swag. He walked through the all-black campus as if there was absolutely nothing separating him from us. And he brought that same genuine ease and enthusiasm to the classroom. Daniel was creative and someone I could relate to. We'd sit, talk about my work, and the art of writing. He asked questions that forced me to consider the world differently. I got great feedback on my writing, and I wasn't expected to be anyone else but myself. The class wasn't about who could write the best among us, we weren't competing. It felt like a cool club of people who appreciated self-expression.

Daniel required us to turn in a poem every week. This was my first time applying any sort of discipline to my writing. Every Wednesday I would come to class with my poem ready. We each read our own to the class, and Daniel would offer constructive critique. Until that class I believed poems had to rhyme. I thought rhyming made poetry easier to digest and remember. I'd labor for hours trying to match syllables, hoping to make my point without losing the rhythm. Then one day I recited a poem that I could not get to rhyme the way I wanted it to. In fact, it did not rhyme at all, it was purely my free-flowing thoughts. When I was done reading, the class was clapping and Daniel gave me a perfect score.

The response inspired me to go deeper and to take risks beyond the rhyming confines I held myself to as a writer.

I wrote a poem about an abortion.

Cynthia (not her real name) was a girl I'd met at a party. She was funny, smart, and cute. We became involved at a time when I was enjoying my freedom, and having sex was something I did when I could, just because I could. I wasn't after any one woman and generally felt inexperienced in the area of romance. I wanted to figure out what I loved about women and sex. We were having fun hanging out and spending time, friends with benefits at best. I was trying to climax and I think that's all she was looking for too.

She texted me, "I'm pregnant."

Caught completely off guard, I responded, "A baby?"

"Yes fool, don't worry. I'm handling it tomorrow. I just thought it would be wrong if I didn't tell you before I did it."

I don't think she ever considered keeping it. I knew it would be a disaster for us and for the child, but I would've felt crazy telling her she had to get an abortion. If it was something she was truly against, I would've had to eat that and deal with it.

"I'm tired, but I just wanted to let you know it was handled. I'm going to lay low for a few weeks. I'll check in on you soon."

I felt everything but relief. I felt irresponsible. I'd let this happen.

When I handed in the poem about the abortion, I asked if I could recite mine last. I wanted as much time as possible before sharing. I thought Daniel and my classmates would judge me. I felt crazy writing about something like an abortion, but the experience wasn't something I could ignore. Part of me hoped someone in the class had been through it before (although I'd never wish this situation upon anyone), and maybe they would pull me aside and talk to me after class. But better than any advice or conversation, they all gave me hugs afterward, starting with Daniel. As the period closed, Daniel gave me a note on my delivery: "The next time you recite this, do it with those same inflections, but say it just a tad slower. Take an extra breath to help you with the pace. People need to feel the weight of each word, the gravity of the circumstance. You're incredible."

It felt like I was coming alive, one Wednesday at a time.

The semester was going well, but I was feeling unsettled after the abortion happened. I began getting the urge to move away. I loved the thought of possibly transferring to another school and starting out in a new environment. The urge was also surprising to me as I was the one who complained about moving so much in the past . . . Maybe I was used to it now.

Or maybe I wanted to run.

The age of social media makes it hard to get over someone. These days the easiest way to relight an old flame or start a new one is uploading the right picture onto Facebook or Instagram. Our lives are so webbed together in online communities. Even if you don't see that person directly, you'll see their best friend, their mother, them in a picture with someone you didn't even think they knew. And if that's not enough, Facebook has a daily pop-up message on users' home screens that shows posts they put up from previous years. I've learned to use it as a housekeeping tool, quickly dusting away with the click of a finger posts that have become emotionally insignificant.

I always saw Sequoyah's pictures on Facebook. She was my prom date in high school. I'll explain. Sequoyah and I met in the eighth grade. She sat right in front of me in math at Hugo Owens Middle School in Chesapeake while I was there for the first half of the year. I loved to talk and she loved to laugh so we'd pass the time keeping each other entertained, but we rarely spoke outside of school. I left for Germany at the end of the first semester. The weekend before we left, Elise and I had a going-away party. I invited Sequoyah, but she didn't come. I didn't see her again until I returned to Chesapeake for my senior year of high school.

My family moved from New Jersey back to Virginia in 2004, just before the start of my senior year. Sequoyah and I were dating by the first game of basketball season in December. Although she was in a relationship with someone, we just had a connection. There was something familiar about her that I appreciated. Still, in May, a couple weeks after prom, we decided we were better off as friends.

Sequoyah and I were living in the same city but going to different colleges. We'd go a few weeks without speaking, both seeing other people, but we always found a way to get back in touch with each other. Over the years, she was there for me through difficult times with my parents and losing Teo. I wouldn't have gotten the job selling cell phone accessories at the mall without Sequoyah letting me use her car to drive to the interview. Our bond was genuine, we both brought passion to the relationship, but separately we had our own issues. We were guarded; she was hurt from her father being incarcerated and I held a similar knot in my heart with Dana in jail at the same time. We both wanted them there during our senior year of high school. We both feared getting hurt by letting someone get too close. We didn't have clear boundaries; one day we were, "I want to see you" and the next day we were, "Oh, I was busy." We were young, with our entire lives ahead of us. It was clear that we didn't consider our relationship the most important thing in the world.

In May of 2007, Sequoyah and I went to my aunt Daiquiri's house to see my cousin Jewell off to prom. Jewell looked amazing and we all were filled with the spirit of celebration. It reminded me of our night. Another friend who played on the junior varsity basketball team my senior year was attending the same prom too. He gave me cash and asked me to book a room for him at the hotel across the street from the venue since he wasn't yet eighteen. Sequoyah came with me, and after getting the keys we went to the room to check it out. It wasn't the honeymoon suite but I got him what he requested. After coming out of the bathroom, I locked my eyes on Sequoyah and walked toward her while drying my hands with a towel. Before I could speak, she kissed me. We could not keep our hands off each other. It was passionate, it was desire, it was the sound of Maxwell singing "This Woman's Work" and at the end it was just us. We knew this didn't mean we were back in a relationship. We'd been here before.

I drove her back to her car, we kissed again, and we went our separate ways.

At the end of the semester, Daniel held an awards ceremony. Everyone was given a superlative and the one he honored me with was "The Most Transparent Writer." No one had ever called me transparent. In fact, I'd worked hard up until that point to be the one who didn't show what he was going through. I lived by a "never let them see you sweat" motto. Yet, as I stood in front of the room of upperclassmen, I held the award for transparency. I was being recognized for being myself. I felt like my experiences and the courage to share them openly paid off for a greater cause and I was proud.

As summer arrived that year, I wanted to have more fun, money, and I still wanted to transfer schools. NSU was a good start, but Joey, Corey, and a few other friends were transferring to Virginia Commonwealth University one hour away in Richmond. Though I was nervous my GPA would stop me from being accepted as a transfer student, my plan was to go too. The new environment was going to be fresh ground for me to grow.

Then . . . "Robert, I'm six weeks pregnant." Those words came off Sequoyah's lips like the slow drip of molasses.

It was July of 2007. I couldn't believe it. She said she was on birth control, that she'd been on it. She also admitted that there was a gap where she switched methods, and that gap was in May when we were together. I was stunned. She made it clear that she wanted to keep the baby and I was clear that I was not ready to be a father.

I loved Sequoyah. I knew she wanted to keep the baby. And it was decided from there. Sequoyah and I fell into this "we're stuck with each other" kind of relationship. Sometimes we called it love.

I never even applied to VCU, knowing I couldn't leave then. My friends spent the summer moving up to Richmond without me.

I wanted to get a job before I broke the news to my mother. We were in a good place. Our relationship had improved greatly and I thought this news would ruin that. After about two weeks

I got a job at a call center handling service contract issues for General Electric. We handled repair requests that came through our department for refrigerators, microwaves, ranges, and other kitchen appliances under warranty. I started at fourteen dollars per hour. After I finished training, I went over to my mom's house to drop the bomb.

"Mom, Sequoyah's pregnant," I said, expecting her face to fill up with anger and disappointment. Yet she was surprisingly calm.

"I knew it. I had a feeling that's what you were coming over here to tell me. God showed me in my dream." After a deep breath and a long pause, she looked in my eyes and continued, "So you're going to be a father, huh?"

"Yes, I'm going to be a father," I replied with my voice cracking.

"Don't worry, Robert, you'll learn how to be a good one."

Sequoyah's mom seemed less understanding than mine. One day Sequoyah called to tell me that they had been arguing, one thing led to another, and eventually Sequoyah needed to find somewhere else to stay. She didn't say why, but I think it was because she was pregnant. I felt like her situation was my fault.

"Mom, she doesn't have anywhere else to go." I felt crazy letting the words flow from my lips but I knew my mom was the only person I could ask. This was her first grandbaby and he was going to need a safe place to live. Sequoyah moved into my parents' house immediately, and I subsequently moved in too. If I had to live in their house again, this wasn't the way

I wanted to do it. I definitely didn't want to move back while being broke, unwed with a baby on the way, and no plan for my future. Sequoyah had a room upstairs in the house. I took the room downstairs by the garage.

Working at the call center was okay, but it was boring. My passion for college was gone but I stayed in because "it looked good." I can't remember one class, one assignment, or professor from the fall 2007 semester. My focus was on making money. The more hours I worked the bigger my check. The steady money coming in was the only comfort I could find as my son's birth was only months away. Still, I'd sit at my desk, thinking about how the next twenty years of my life would play out. That guy stuck in a cubicle doing work that brought no joy for the rest of my life was not who I wanted to be.

Meanwhile, NSU's campus wasn't the same without Joey and my other friends. On the weekends I started taking trips to Richmond to visit them at VCU. My priorities weren't about what I needed to do to prepare for fatherhood. I just wanted to party and be around my boys.

One night in Richmond my friends and I were planning to hit this party. With my facial hair I looked much older than twenty and I had little worry of getting carded when walking into the liquor store. I bought a bottle of Rain vodka. It came in a curvy clear bottle with a blue top, which I thought looked cool. Anyway, we started pregaming. This is when you get as buzzed as possible at home for significantly less money than buying drinks at the club. The goal is to be sober enough to leave where you are and make it to the party. I did ten shots of vodka that night before we left the house.

I liked to drive whenever I went out to have fun, that way I could leave whenever I wanted. So I got behind the wheel of my new ride, a white 1995 Chevy Blazer. It was a gift from my aunt Daiquiri after my Honda broke down for good. I was following one of my boys down Broad Street, the busiest road in Richmond, when I lost him and had no idea where the party was. I looked down into my lap for a moment to grab my phone when I heard the two friends riding with me scream, "Whoa. Whoa. Whoa. Rob, chill!"

By the time I slammed on the brakes, the front end of my truck was already hitting against the back of the small two-door coupe in front of me.

Adrenaline rushed through my body. I knew I was in the wrong. I knew I had been drinking. I couldn't move. A short white woman quickly jumped from the driver's seat of the car to check for any damage to her car. I was going about thirty-five miles per hour at the time I hit the brakes, and luckily there wasn't any real damage. She waved me off, got back in the car, and pulled off. I was so relieved that I sped off down Broad Street, wanting to get as far away from her and the accident as possible. But, as it turned out, I ran a red light.

Blue lights were behind me within seconds. Things were about to get bad. Again.

I pulled over and parked between two industrial buildings. The cop was a young Latino man who ran my license and registration and asked if I had been drinking. "Yes, Officer, I had two beers." I figured he'd appreciate the honesty, even if it wasn't the full truth. We were college kids on a college campus. He asked us to get out of the car, instructed me to come to one side of the street and my friends across from me to the other. I chose to do the field sobriety test. If he brought out the Breathalyzer, I knew it would be over. The officer asked me to recite the alphabet starting with the letter C and ending at Q. I walked on a line with my knees slightly bent trying to use my athletic past to my advantage. I was as cooperative as possible in hopes of getting out of the ugly situation. Another police car showed up. I sat on the curb while the officers conferred off to the side, out of earshot. It felt like hours, sitting there, waiting to learn my fate.

"I'm not going to arrest you tonight because everything checks out on your registration and license. You are free to go. Stay safe out there." The officer gave me a ticket for the hit-and-run (which he had witnessed) and for running the red light. He didn't mention the beer or alcohol at all.

Now another court date was looming over me. The last one ended with me in jail.

I vomited as soon as I got back to my boy's house. All of my emotions from the evening finally caught up with me. I couldn't hold it in any longer. I wasn't cool. The way I was living wasn't cool. And I was just tired.

I had a son coming into this world soon, another life I was going to be responsible for. It was going to be my job to teach him how to properly throw a football, how to treat women, tie a tie, be a man, yet I still took ten shots of vodka and got behind the wheel of a car.

What if that minor fender bender hadn't been minor? What if the damage had been fatal? What if instead of sitting on the curb, I ended up lying in the morgue? Or in jail for killing someone else?

I thought about Dana again. Funny how he always came to mind when I found myself in trouble. I wondered if he was that age when he got his first DUI?

If I refused to take ownership of everything in my life, and do it quickly, I would always be miserable. And worse, as a father I would be choosing my hurt over my son's happiness. I couldn't let that happen. I needed to be better, not just for him but for myself. My head swirled. My heart ached. I felt both lost and hopeful. A miracle was coming, I just had to make sure I was ready to receive it.

January 19, 2008

Robert B. Hillman Jr. was born: 6 pounds, 10 ounces, and 19.5 inches long.

I was terrified.

The doctor handed him directly to me. He didn't cry or look away. He felt warm and wet, and smelled a little like everything he'd been swimming in for the last eight months. He opened his eyes; they were deep brown and so innocent, so caring, and so pure. I had never seen eyes so uncorrupted. He didn't know what disappointment felt like. He wasn't bitter from heartbreak. He held no resentment toward anyone for what they hadn't done. He was brand-new and my job became not to mess him up. We stared at each other and it was like he could see inside my heart and through to my soul. I felt like he could see my shame, every lie, mistake, and all the times I had fallen short. It was as if he could see it all, yet to him it meant nothing. I was holding him and that meant he was fine.

I felt a surge of energy. It was love. Real love. I wanted to feel worthy. Like I deserved to keep this powerful force close.

I wanted my son to live in a perfect world. However, in the real world, I needed to grow up.

As a child I imagined myself as a father providing a loving household, teaching my family the virtues of life, and growing old cherishing our bond. We would be best friends. He would be brought up the right way with both parents happily in the household. The way you see it in the movies. We'd have the two-story white house with a matching picket fence and a dog, a Labrador retriever. While all of this was nice to imagine, I felt so far from actually achieving any of it.

What kind of father would I be?

Would I be closer to my son than my father Dana was to me?

Would my son think of me as his hero, this great man— whose name he shared?

A person's legacy is the collection of their decisions. The work, wisdom, and gifts that they want to pass down. My son's birth was my first time ever considering legacy, and my first time deciding that it was time to establish the foundation that mine would rest on. Sure, the call center wouldn't work for twenty years, but what was working for me?

I sold cell phone accessories.
I cut hair in a barbershop.
I sold shoes and moved boxes in Target.
I took calls at the call center.

Do I stay in college, collecting debt, working to provide, and have limited benefits? Or do I try something else?

College was a dream of mine, but with a newborn son, I needed to be practical and earn some money.

Now was the time to work. Now was the time to sacrifice.

CHAPTER FOUR

Learning My New Life

I joined the navy.

At three months old, Robert was diagnosed with craniosynostosis, a condition in which one or more of the fibrous sutures in an infant's skull prematurely fuses and basically turns into bone. When it happens, the growth pattern of the child's skull visibly changes. In some cases, the skull provides the necessary space for the growing brain, but results in an abnormal head shape and abnormal facial features. In other cases, like my son's, it does not effectively provide enough space for the growing brain. So from there things can gradually get worse, like increased intracranial pressure, visual or sleeping impairment, eating difficulties, or an impairment of mental development that could lead to significant reduction in IQ. Basically, his head was shaped like a football. Thankfully, Robert wasn't in any pain, but Sequoyah and I both wanted to do something right away to help him.

We first decided we needed to get a second opinion. The doctors informed us of a few options to correct Robert's condition. We could let things play out and observe his development and try our best to address any issues as they arose. Or we could explore a "cosmetic" reconstructive surgery that would fix the fused sutures to avoid potential problems. Surgery seemed best but neither Sequoyah nor I had the money to afford a procedure like that. Even worse, I didn't have health insurance. My son wasn't even a year old, but I was beginning to feel like I was about to let him down in a major way. The doctors told Sequoyah and me that it would be safer to get the surgery around his nine-month mark. I felt a brief moment of relief knowing we had time to prepare. But I left the hospital with a deep pain in the pit of my stomach.

I stopped working at the call center altogether. It didn't offer medical insurance and I needed a job that did. So the search for an employer with good benefits was on. I went to job fairs anywhere I could find them, looked in the Classified section of the newspaper, and drove around dressed interview-ready with spare ties on the back seat of my car. This wasn't my first time looking for a job, but it was the first time I remember feeling like the work I did had to support someone other than myself. I now had to make enough money to cover my son's needs and my own.

One day I got so fed up with job searching that I walked

right into the air force recruiting office. As a child, growing up with a dad who served made me detest the thought of ever joining the military. I didn't want that on-the-move every few years lifestyle for my family. But I was no longer a child. I walked into the office that day as a father trying to make a way. I knew everybody in the service got paid consistently on the first and fifteenth of every month, plus full benefits. I wanted that to be me. I sat there silently; the recruiting center was swamped with people and it felt as if no one noticed me walk in. After waiting ten minutes, a half-interested recruiter asked, "How can I help you?" I got to the point quickly.

"My name is Robert Hillman. I'm twenty, I have a son, and I'd like to join the air force. But first I have a question: Is there any way to guarantee I'll be stationed in Virginia?"

"No, you'll go where we need you. Your duty station will depend on the type of job you qualify for, but I can tell you now, chances are slim you'll start in Virginia." His tone gave off a "you're dreaming, kid" kind of vibe.

I sat there for a moment, wondering what it would be like to be stationed somewhere like Oklahoma, miles away from my son and family. Before I spoke again, the blunt recruiter continued. "You should probably go next door and talk to a navy recruiter. You may have better chances with them since Norfolk is their headquarters."

Wait . . . the navy has a headquarters? And it's in Norfolk? That's all I needed to know. I thanked the air force recruiter for his time and walked out.

When I walked into the navy recruiting office Petty Officer Gonzalez was the first person to greet me. I'd taken no more than three steps before he invited me to have a seat at his desk. He started out, "So what brings you into the office today?" I repeated my script.

"My name is Robert Hillman. I'm twenty, I have a son, and I'd like to join the navy. But first I have a question: Is there any way to guarantee I'll be stationed in Virginia?"

Gonzalez smiled at me as he leaned back in his chair. "Well, I'm glad you're interested in serving. You came to the right branch. The Hampton Roads area happens to be the headquarters for our entire Atlantic Fleet. Though the final decision is dependent on a few factors, there are some things you can do to increase your chances of getting the duty station that you want." From there he had my attention.

My next inquiry was about their benefits and pay. I explained to him the type of surgery my son needed and asked if it would be covered under their insurance plan. Before promising anything, Gonzalez said he would do some research to verify the coverage. I told him that I would join immediately if the operation would be fully insured. We talked for a few more minutes about the next steps and how the process of transforming from civilian to service member worked. I left feeling like that new path could bring some good into my life.

A couple of days went by before I got the call from Gonzalez. I didn't focus on anything he said beyond "Tricare Prime will cover your son's surgery." That's all I wanted to hear, and in the seconds following, I made my decision to join. I knew my life was going to change. I knew there could be deployments and long work hours. I also knew that I didn't have much to lose and that my son had everything to gain.

Three weeks later, on April 23, 2008, I started my first day of basic training.

The navy has only one location for boot camp: the Naval Station Great Lakes. The Recruit Training Command (RTC) is positioned thirty-six miles north of Chicago, just along the western shore of Lake Michigan. The weather was freezing cold with snow falling and covering the ground when I arrived. This would be home for the next nine weeks as I became indoctrinated into life as a navy sailor. Time seemed to move lightning fast during my first few days at the RTC. It's called "P Week." P Week does not count toward the official eight weeks of boot camp, but from the moment I stepped off of the bus it was clear that the training had begun. The first drill we were taught is the position of attention. We were instructed to bring our heels together sharply on line, with our toes pointing out equally, forming an angle of forty-five degrees. Face front, head up, shoulders square, chest lifted, legs straight but without locking the knees. We were told to stand there, to shut up, and not to speak unless someone asked us a question.

By the end of P week, we were assigned to a "recruit division." It was a total of eighty men, and they housed us in navy-style dormitories, which we called "ships." My division had members from many different places—New York, Vermont, Maine, Texas, California, the Philippines, Jamaica, Florida, Alabama, and more. Seeing so many different faces reminded me of the melting pot that makes up America. I did not know what to expect from these guys, but I did know the key to first-week survival in any new place: don't make yourself stand out. Through early conversations and whispers I learned about the Delayed Entry Program (DEP), which trained people on what to expect when arriving at basic. Most of the people in my division had participated in the program for more than six months before joining. As they quizzed each other, preparing to be questioned at any moment, I instantly realized that they knew more information than I did, and I avoided speaking at all. *What are the general orders?* I don't know. *What is the complete chain of command?* I have no idea. *Recite the sailor's creed.* Huh? Those terms meant nothing to me.

From the first morning until our last day, the RTC schedule would be 0600–2200 (6 a.m.–10 p.m.). Every day, no exceptions. Lights out at 2200. My three recruit division commanders (RDCs) were Chief Petty Officer Little, Petty Officer First Class Bynum, and Petty Officer First Class Canty. Chief Little was in charge and his word was final. We all stood at attention and screamed "Yes, sir" loudly to show that we understood. After a week of observation, the RDCs selected recruit leaders, known as "recruit petty officers" (RPOs), with the top two being Recruit Chief Petty Officer (RPOC) and Assistant Recruit Chief Petty Officer (AROC). To earn the RPO position you had to be deemed "squared away" by the RDCs. This meant ironing your uniform, making the bed properly, and knowing your information.

RPOs are seen as authority figures among the other recruits in the division. When RPOs receive an order from the RDCs, they are responsible for making sure the division executes the mission and assignment efficiently. I was not selected for an RPO position. I did not come to basic training to be responsible for anyone but myself. I kept a low profile. Before I'd arrived I could barely help myself, and I didn't think I'd be helping anyone else by asking to lead. I spent my time listening, reading the manual, observing the people around me, writing letters, and thinking about Robert Jr.

Aside from the intensive first-week physical conditioning, we were also required to take our initial swim qualifications. This meant jumping from a twenty-foot platform into a pool and swimming the length, end to end, one time. I'd been swimming since I was six years old and had no fears about the qualification. Most of the division did well, with no more than five people failing. Newell, who was chosen as AROC, was within that few. For the remainder of the week in the classroom we focused on rank/rate recognition, rape awareness, equal opportunities, sexual harassment and fraternization, and the navy core values: Honor, Courage, and Commitment. I caught on to things fast, so I started speaking up often, and by the end of the week I was beginning to stand out. The RDCs were learning my name. Week two began with everyone in our division getting their wisdom teeth pulled, that is, everyone except me. The entire division was drugged up with swollen faces when it came time to march back to our ship from dental. Chief Little looked at me and said, "Hillman, you got AROC. I'll get them in formation, you call it out and get us home." Without a word, I lined up alongside the division in AROC position and began counting the cadence as soon as I heard Chief Little issue the forward march command.

Over the next few weeks I often found myself studying my peers. There were so many different types of people in basic training. Some were older and some were younger but everyone endured the process in their own way. Some cried their way through while others complained. Some worked harder to become better and others found ways to fake injuries and quit. It was interesting to observe how a change of environment could reveal a person's true character. I didn't allow myself to have opinions about the work I was doing. I just committed to doing what I was asked to the best of my ability.

It was a few days before graduating from basic training when the RDCs called me into their office. Standing silently at attention, I listened as I was told I would be recognized during our ceremony as top of my class, graduating with honors and promoted from E1 to E2. There were eleven divisions and almost one thousand people would be graduating that day. Only nine were recognized as honor graduates. I was the only one out of that nine representing the division who won the Captain's Cup, the culminating event representing the end of boot camp.

Damn, that was the feeling I imagined a successful college career would bring, walking across the stage with my degree. Instead, I was a sailor. I felt like a new person, more equipped to be a stable, income-earning father with benefits. Not to mention, I was in the best physical shape of my life.

The day of graduation I woke up excited about walking across the stage in full dress. My mom, Elise, Sequoyah, and Robert Jr. flew in from Virginia and would be in attendance. The graduation went smoothly and in grand fashion. The families of honor graduates had special seating beside the captain and other ranking officers, and the large ceremony hall was filled with people. My mom was the first face I spotted as our division marched in.

Our time with family was limited to a few hours after the graduation ceremony. Robert and I took pics in the mall. We got food, and I was back in my rack by lights out at 2200. The only thing I could think about was how good it felt to hold Robert; he was growing fast.

The next day I boarded a plane headed to class A school in Meridian, Mississippi. Before joining the military, each person has to take the Armed Services Vocational Aptitude Battery (ASVAB), a multiple-choice test used to determine qualification for enlistment. Your score on this test determines the type of jobs the navy will offer you. I scored a seventy-three out of a possible ninety-nine. I was offered four different jobs and I chose the rate of Storekeeper (SK). "Rate" describes a person's job; mine was SK. "Rank" describes a person's position in the chain of command; mine was E2 or "seaman apprentice." I was SKSA Hillman.

Reporting to class A school meant it was time for some technical training.

My focus was to earn top of my class so that I could pick my orders and first duty station. In between training sessions, I passed time reading and writing in my journal. I read a book written by Myles Munroe titled *The Fatherhood Principle*. I bought it while visiting the Navy Exchange store on base.

"All men are fathers," the back cover read. "The inherent purpose of all men is fatherhood . . . although every man is called to be a father, knowing how to live in this purpose is not automatic. We must understand the characteristics and master the skills of fatherhood." I read on as the book talked about exhibiting qualities of leadership, integrity, responsibility, and obedience to the ultimate Father, our Father God in heaven. The language was concise and the message very compelling. Dr. Munroe explained how a man can become a provider, nourisher, protector, teacher, leader, and developer. I turned the pages eager to soak up wisdom, excited to learn the keys of fatherhood. My lack of closeness with Dana inspired a fiery passion within me to be the complete opposite with Robert. I wanted to be hands-on and present, not an every-once-in-a-while father.

After five weeks at A school I was out of there. Mission accomplished! My grades and test scores put me in the top 5 percent of my class. I excelled on the PT test and made sure I did everything the petty officers in charge asked of me. I was given the chance to pick my own orders. The options were San Diego, Hawaii, or Virginia Beach. I didn't even know there was a base in Virginia Beach, but I instantly said, "That's *it*! Virginia Beach is the one for me. Thank you, I'll take it." And just like that, I was headed back home to the Hampton Roads area, Virginia Beach, only fifteen minutes from Chesapeake.

In the first week of September, at nine months old, Robert had his surgery. Sending your infant into surgery is an indescribable fear that I'd never wish upon even my worst enemy. But Little Rob pulled through like a champ, without complications. He was in a lot of pain, his head completely wrapped in bandages, on an IV, with cords and machines hooked up to so many parts of his body. I wanted to trade places with him; it hurt seeing his face swollen to the point where he couldn't open his own eyes or his mouth to cry. I stood there holding his forearm. It felt like Teo all over again. Except this time, I *was* praying, I was asking God to make sure my son would live and be okay.

I was stationed in Virginia Beach, my command, VFA-131, an F/A-18 aircraft strike fighter squadron. On the first day I checked in I was informed that we were in line to do two back-to-back deployments onboard the USS *Dwight D. Eisenhower* (*Ike*). The first one was slated to start in the beginning of 2009, just six months away. The *Eisenhower* is a $4.5 billion nuclear-powered aircraft carrier that stretches 1,092 feet and houses roughly 5,000 sailors. It's like a floating city inhabited by fathers, mothers, grandparents, brothers, and sisters. Ships like the *Ike* are considered some of our military's strongest weapons due to their many capabilities on the sea.

The day before my twenty-first birthday, on September 16, 2008, the *Ike* departed Naval Station Norfolk for carrier qualifications. I woke up on the morning of the seventeenth, worked out in the gym, and walked into our storeroom/office by 0530. I celebrated the rest of the day with fifteen hours of work. I reflected on nearly being arrested the year before for running the light and the hit-and-run. Thankfully, I walked away from that courtroom with both tickets being thrown out and not back in jail. I thought to myself: *Better to be on the boat making money than home drinking, spending money, or creating headaches for later.*

The next couple weeks on the *Ike* were smooth. I spent time learning my environment, the different divisions aboard the ship, and how to do my job at sea. I was assigned a mentor in 6'2" Petty Officer Third Class Schneider from Florida. Schneider wanted me to know two things about him: 1) He knew his shit when it came to the job. 2) He was getting out of the navy as soon as we got off deployment. I followed him closely and he taught me as if I were his protégé. Anytime I had a problem he had the solution. He would quiz me to make sure I was retaining the things he taught. But no one could teach me how to respond to what happened next.

On October 4, a shipmate was killed when he was hit by a plane, at 8:16 p.m., during a training exercise off the coast of North Carolina. I was fresh out of the shower in the berthing where we slept after work. The TV was tuned to the flight deck. The flight deck is where aircraft take off and land from the ship; it feels like a miniature airport on water. It happened in a flash, and I wish I could've looked away. I did not know the sailor personally, but I knew I walked on that same flight deck at least five times a day. We are told to be on high alert anytime the ship is at sea. But preparing to watch someone die? There was no alert. Only responses, stunned reactions from people who were on the deck while it happened, the shipmates who had to walk step by step retrieving his remains, and those of us who could not believe what we had just seen. I climbed in my rack thankful for my safety and praying I could find a way to rest without replaying the vision over and over again in my mind. Tomorrow was another day of work, and everyone was sharper. You could tell that nobody wanted that mistake to happen ever again.

After twenty-one days at sea we were back at home. Robert was healing from surgery. His face was still swollen in areas but much of it was reduced. His eyes were open and his mouth was able to make the most beautiful smile. I was so happy to have him in my arms.

When I was a child and my family left one place for another, I tried not to look back at that time period with sadness. I learned how to say goodbye quickly and without any emotion. But saying goodbye was so much harder now. I was leaving my son.

I was scared to leave, scared to return to life changing and being completely different without me. Robert was starting to stand up on his own two feet. It was beautiful to see him learning to walk and being so resilient. I knew he would be a professional at walking by the time I got off the ship in six months. Nevertheless, it was time to go.

CHAPTER FIVE

A New Era of Responsibility

In February of 2009 the *Ike* departed Naval Station Norfolk for our scheduled Middle East deployment. We spent the first two weeks onboard the *Ike* cruising at high speeds across the Atlantic Ocean into the Mediterranean Sea. Most nights I did not even feel us moving. In heavy seas we brought as many aircraft as possible within the hangar bar and tied everything else down on the flight deck. It was amazing to see the waves rising and crashing over the deck. But it was scary at times knowing the water could rise up to sixty feet. I was in awe, knowing that the ocean made waves that huge, and storms that could rock a ship of our size.

The key to surviving life on an aircraft carrier is to develop a solid routine. At all hours someone is working and the time is split into two shifts, day check and night check. Day check works from 0600–1800 and nights from 1800-0600. My job as an aviation Storekeeper (SK) meant helping the planes in our squadron maintain their mission readiness; we had fourteen total. I was assigned to day check and spent my time ordering parts, communicating with the different divisions about their needs, running errands to pick up support material, and counting inventory. Our SK work center was in a small 10 × 15 shipboard storeroom. Each day the work is physically challenging and mentally demanding. Flexibility and a positive attitude are essential, but the upbeat attitude is at times hard to keep up. There were no days off. "Hillman, it's all about individual motivation, ability, and work ethic. They will determine how far you advance." Schneider always reminded me to stay sharp. And I did. My routine was built on using my time wisely and setting minimal expectations. If I wasn't working then I was writing or doing some physical exercise.

My shift each day usually ended by 1930 hours. I would be asleep in my rack by 2200. Our squadrons' berthing (sleeping area) was located on the "O3" level, just below the flight deck. The deck had four catapults to launch planes and four arresting gear cables to retrieve them after flight missions. We slept behind the arresting gear, and tried to ignore its thunderous and at times screeching sounds. It's an area that makes it hard to get a good night's sleep. Fifty-thousand-pound aircraft landing within a few feet overhead. When I could not rest, I sat up and watched television. Our programming was provided through the Ameri-

can Forces Network (AFN), a broadcast service operated by the
United States Armed Forces. In most cases, a few channels were
available. One with movies, another with programs like sitcoms
and series, and the third channel offered training programming
for ship personnel. Any extra channels show activity on the
flight deck, news, and occasional sporting events. Our favorite
nights were when they aired NBA games. I stayed out of the
way whenever someone was watching political news coverage.
Those conversations always got heated and I didn't think it was
worth the energy.

Obama was always a hot-button issue.

*"My fellow citizens: I stand here today humbled by the task
before us, grateful for the trust you've bestowed, mindful of the
sacrifices borne by our ancestors."*

I remember sitting quietly, listening as President Barack
Obama opened our nation's forty-fourth Presidential Inauguration.

"How the fuck is this guy president? What is really happening in this country?" I overheard one of the chiefs say. "His name
sounds like one of the guys we're headed to drop bombs on,"
another officer joked as they all laughed. Their response wasn't
about patriotism, it was clear they did not approve of President
Obama as a person. I, on the other hand was amazed to see him.
I approved of him graduating from Harvard and Columbia. I
approved of his impressive track record as a US senator and his
advocacy for healthcare and education. I adored his beautiful
wife, Michelle, their family, and his dope jump shot. I even had
dreams of somehow being invited to the White House to meet
them.

On his campaign, then senator Obama encouraged a new hope for change within Americans and for the US system of democracy. Before him I never thought of any politician as inspiring. I knew of reverends Jesse Jackson and Al Sharpton. I admired Representative John Lewis and his civil rights sacrifice. I related to their causes and was aware of how the work they did impacted people. Still, Barack Obama was the first to seize my full attention. I did not want to assume my superiors' immediate displeasure with our new president was because his race differed from their own. So I kept my mouth shut hoping to hear a legitimate concern or problem that Obama created to receive such aversion from them. Instead, I heard, "We still haven't seen this guy's birth certificate. He's not from this country." From there I tuned the conversation out, I knew it was headed in a ridiculous direction that would be hard to sit through silently. Thank God it was chow time.

Before leaving, I listened to more of the inauguration speech.

Our challenges may be new. The instruments with which we meet them may be new. But those values upon which our success depends—honesty and hard work, courage and fair play, tolerance and curiosity, loyalty and patriotism—these things are old. These things are true. They have been the quiet force of progress throughout our history. What is demanded, then, is a return to these truths. What is required of us now is a new era of responsibility.

—PRESIDENT BARACK OBAMA

Sidenote about Obama:

My first time ever watching the results of an election was in fourth grade, Bill Clinton versus Bob Dole (1996). Our teacher gave us a blank map and offered extra credit if we marked the states red for republican voters and blue if democrats had majority. It was fun, I stayed up coloring each state accordingly as I watched the results unfold with my family. Bill Clinton won and I remember everyone being so happy.

Fast-forward twelve years to election night, November 4, 2008. The candidates were Senator Barack Obama and Senator John McCain. I tuned into CNN to watch the coverage, proud to have submitted my absentee ballot early. This was the first presidential election I ever voted in, and I was praying it counted toward nominating our nation's first black president. While the early results came in I could hear Tupac echoing in my ear . . . "And though it seems evident, we ain't ready to see a black president." The banner across the bottom of the screen changed to signal the final results. The camera was pointed directly at a podium center stage. Our new president Barack Obama emerged holding hands with his wife, First Lady Michelle Obama.

I burst into tears and I couldn't control it. I sat there on the edge of the bed in awe and I cried in my room alone. I truly never expected to see the day when any black person was *the* president of the United States. And even if I had, there was no way my vision could have done Barack Obama justice. He was captivating, convincing, and so relatable.

The next day at work the majority of my coworkers were visibly pissed about the outcome of the election. They remarked on the joy of being on deployment and away from this downhill-headed country. I didn't take anything personally. Barack was president, commander in chief. They didn't have to like it, but he was the boss. Personally, I felt safer being in the service under his term.

Derek Frye was a coworker within my squadron and always had a wise bit to offer. His rate was Aviation Maintenance Administrationman (AZ). "We do everything from A to Z," he joked. SK and AZ departments work hand in hand to manage flight records, log times, inspection upkeep, and overall maintenance. Though Frye arrived at the command two months after I did, it felt like he was the one getting me comfortable with everything while we were deployed. Frye set the tone for a great relationship between the two of us. He nicknamed me Sugar Hill and the moniker quickly caught on within our squadron. The nickname came from the 1994 movie featuring Wesley Snipes.

"Thirteen years, it'll be fourteen in August," he said in between bites after I asked him how long he had been in the service. Frye and I had a lot of time for conversation in our work day and we took full advantage of that. I became his barber the first week into deployment and from there we continued to build a dependable friendship. I listened every time he imparted some wisdom.

"Listen, don't let all that talk in there get to you. I've heard all kinds of crazy shit over the years. I just keep it moving. Don't let this ship or anybody on it drive you crazy. Work hard, the respect will follow. That man Barry O is president, and he earned it the right way. Nobody can destroy that."

On our way to the Arabian Sea, our "area of theater," where we would be anchored for the next few months, we stopped in Marseille, France, for a port of call. We were free to go ashore for a few hours but we had to travel in groups of no less than three. My group was Frye, myself, and SK2 Gray, a cool guy from my division who always had a funny story to tell. Frye and I loved to sit and listen to him rant. Not long after visiting Marseille we were pulling into the Suez Canal, the shortest link between the East and the West. And then, action. On March 21, 2009, our Air Wing launched its first combat missions in support of Operation Enduring Freedom (OEF) from the Arabian Sea. No land was in sight. We were five hundred miles off the coast of Afghanistan aiding the troops there fighting on the ground. Our jets launched off the flight deck in eight-hour intervals and we supported them with the parts, repairs, and replacements they needed to stay in the air. Every day was the same and I began to lose track of the dates on the calendar. I woke up, did my work, ate, and repeated the routine like clockwork. I was beginning to feel drained and unmotivated. "Four more months of this shit." I remember whispering the words under a deep sigh in a dull attempt at self-motivation. Four more months of being with the same people, day . . . after day . . . after day . . . There is no changing ships, flying home for birthdays, funerals, or graduation, and no break. We work together, we eat together, and we live together. If you can't stand your boss or the person that sleeps over you, oh well. If your work center supervisor is a jerk or psycho, there isn't even the escape of going home at the end of the day or having a weekend. The boat is your home and the ship's Plan of the Day (POD) is your schedule. The end.

Deployments create a demanding atmosphere and there are no excuses for not getting an assigned job done. I took pride in finishing tasks early and with quality work. I was being introduced to important people around the ship as I executed orders for the ranking members in our command. I was the perfect young runner, and I always laughed inside when I would receive remarks like, "Wow, you speak so well. Did you go to *some* college?" I knew if I had on a different uniform they wouldn't make those same statements. I don't think it was purposely meant to demean me and it didn't feel like racism . . . but it was not a compliment.

An unexpected compliment did arise on my biannual evaluation. My maintenance officer evaluated me with the status of "Early Promote" which meant I qualified to take the test for advancement from E3 to E4—airman to petty officer third class. There was also a note about a program called STA-21. It's a seaman to admiral program that creates a fair system for outstanding active duty sailors to receive a college education and become commissioned officers. It's one of just five ways an enlisted member can apply to change over to officer ranks. After looking into the program, it highlighted that there were many sailors in the service who would make incredible officers . . . but much like in civilian society there were program restrictions, educational background qualifiers, financial concerns, and other reasons they did not apply. This program was created to fill the gap and I took great pride in being introduced to it this early. I did not imagine myself to be a career sailor completing a twenty-year enlistment, but if I did stay in, being an officer would be a much better quality of life.

My dad Frank is a decorated high-ranking army officer and a graduate of the United States Military Academy at West Point. I joined the navy under much different circumstances from him, and I was far from eligible to be a military academy attendee. I was "enlisted" and it didn't matter if I served thirty years and was promoted to the most senior E9 in the fleet, I would still never be on an equal pay scale with even the most junior officer. You can think of it as officers are responsible for roles like leadership and administration, while enlisted do the less desirable grunt work. If you're a sports fan, a comparable analogy would be equating the officers with the coaches and the enlisted with the players.

"Man, nothing great is easy. But the right combination of aptitude, dedication, training, and experience can turn just about anyone into a good leader, officer, or chief. If everyone started at square one, things would look different. Fuck the ASVAB or a degree, fuck pre-sorting people, let's look at how sailors perform once they're actually in the navy." As Gray ended his rant, I figured out quickly that not everyone thought commissioning programs were the best way to go. Frye and Gray didn't care about being officers, the first class petty officers in line to become chiefs weren't impressed, and the chiefs thought it was a distraction from work. They thought chief was the honorable way to go and the sentiment was echoed louder when I met the command master chief of our Air Wing, Jeffrey Garber. CMC Garber was responsible for the enlisted members in all nine Air Wing squadrons, and he worked hand in hand with CMC Washington at my command. In their eyes I was on the "fast track" and could follow in the footsteps of men like them who rose to the top of the ranks. Men like my Papa, who was a chief. I considered their words and held on to my STA-21 application. I would not be eligible to apply until I had been on active duty for at least four years. I planned to build it as my career unfolded.

The morning of June 20, the ship was stunned with horrible news. CMC Garber was found unresponsive in his stateroom at approximately 0815. A medical emergency was declared, and medical personnel were on the scene within minutes. All efforts to revive CMC Garber were unsuccessful, and by 0823 the forty-three-year-old man who considered my path "the fast track" was pronounced dead. I remember him stopping by to talk to our maintenance officer throughout the flight schedule each day, making jokes with CMC Washington and the other chiefs, always showing love to us young sailors working hard.

"Across the entire Strike Group, we admired Commander Master Chief Garber's professionalism, but we also, on a personal level, genuinely liked him," said Rear Admiral Kurt W. Tidd, Commander, Carrier Strike Group 8. "His passing leaves a hole in our family. We out here at sea were Jeff's 'other' family: the family he spent so many hours and days and years with over the course of his navy career. We were the family that he dedicated so much of his life to serving. Today it is his family back home in Virginia and Nebraska who are very much in our thoughts and prayers. Jeff gave each of us, every day, the full measure of his joy and devotion. We will miss him." Seven days later we honored CMC Garber's life with an underway memorial service.

July 6, 2009, the *Ike* was officially "relieved" by the USS *Ronald Reagan* and their carrier Air Wing group. We were finally heading home and I said prayers of safety as we did our official "pass by" the morning the *Reagan* arrived within sight of our ship. The mission was successful, we accomplished what we came to do. Aircraft from our Air Wing flew more than two thousand sortie missions in support of OEF in Afghanistan.

July 14, 2009, the *Ike* pulled into Lisbon, Portugal, for a three-day port of call. Our "liberty crew" as we called ourselves was consistent: Frye, Gray, and Sugar Hill. "Liberty" is what sailors call off-time. I stuck with this crew because we talked about family, sports, and drank cognac. When we were off of the ship, work did not matter. In fact, the only thing that mattered to me in Lisbon was going back home to my son in Virginia.

My mind created a panic with the thought of returning home in a few weeks. I was used to being gone now and I was sure my family had a whole system that worked with me being absent. I did not want to speak to anyone about my fear. But the more I held my anxiety in, the more scenarios I created with my imagination.

The closer the days got, the harder it was fighting excitement and building expectations for being reunited.

July 30, 2009, the *Ike* returned to Norfolk after our five-month deployment. Coming home was hard. While I was gone Robert stayed with my mom every other week. So he was still very close to her and much more familiar being at my parents' house than with me alone. I moved in with my cousin Tori (Aunt Daiquiri's daughter) and we lived in Holly Point, a neighborhood in Chesapeake. Growing up, my mom, Elise, and I lived in a neighborhood nearby called Arbor Glen. We would ride by the back side of Holly Point to get to school; the complex had a tall white fence surrounding it. At the entrance of the neighborhood was a guard at the gate. As a kid you ride by feeling like only important people must live there. I was happy to have my cousin as a roommate and I enjoyed being home with my son. We got along well after he got a chance to feel me out again. With him I felt my heart opening up. I felt present and necessary.

When it came to dating, things still felt pointless. I wasn't looking for love. I wanted someone to come home to. I went on dates, met women online through social media. I even let some friends play matchmaker for me. I found some sparks with women, but nothing materialized into lasting relationships. In each situation we wanted comfort and we traded food, sex, and cuddling as currency. I didn't have many men whom I felt comfortable talking to about dating. I wanted someone older to talk to about the things that were happening relationship-wise and to help me navigate them. But it was hard for me to open up to older men. I wasn't close in a casual communication sense with either of my dads. Still, I had a strong desire to become my own man. And I was determined to figure out the best way to make it happen.

My definition of manhood was evolving rapidly between fatherhood and life away on the *Ike*. If I was asked a year prior what I thought being "the man" was, I would say it meant you were the one in control, the guy on top, leading and answering to no one. I was wrong. Being a man means having the awareness to recognize a negative habit, then exercising the courage to undo it. The biggest lesson in my manhood studies was the importance of not getting caught up in gender roles. A good person is a good person, their gender has nothing to do with it. I didn't care to be the perfect man. What mattered to me was being a good person, with a good heart.

The direction I chose was simple: I no longer wanted to make decisions that only benefited me. Most of my choices up until that point were heavily influenced by emotion and pride, made in haste, and

> **Every bad habit eventually submits to change when it faces consistent effort.**

leaving me with more damage than peace. Now I was focused on change.

Now was my chance to follow through in this new era of responsibility.

CHAPTER SIX

Proving My Worth

January 2, 2010, the *Ike* departed Naval Station Norfolk for the second of our two scheduled Middle East deployments. Saying goodbye that time was no easier than it was the first, especially now that Robert seemed to be growing faster and faster. I put the thought of missing out on moments with him in the back of my mind. I knew they would be there throughout the next six months, but things would get easier as I got into my daily routine. For this deployment, my goal was to get through it with patience and walk off the boat having grown and matured. I did not want to come back the same; I planned to return stronger.

After passing the test for petty officer third class, I was promoted to LS3. The navy merged two rates together, my previous rate of SK and Postal Clerk (PC), and they formed Logistics Specialist (LS). My job functions and duties within the squadron were still the same, the only change was the title. Within the command I was exceeding expectations and while I had no specific goals for my career, I knew rank was the one thing that gave me options. And I was happy to finally have some.

Much like the first deployment, my attention during free time went to books and exercising in the gym. In the mornings I started my day with silent meditations and an aggressive workout. I was in the gym by 0345 and at work by 0545. Every single day. Being the first one in the shop each morning sends a message that you care about the job and that you're committed to being a leader throughout the day. I decided to always be the first one in. Staying late, helping the next shift transition smoothly, and keeping open lines of communication meant you were dependable and could be trusted to get tasks done.

I began working a new role as the Financial Operations Manager for my squadron. The role was huge and very coveted: it meant I would be responsible for a budget of twenty million dollars. I put my work ethic into overdrive. Though I wasn't a trained accountant, I had no time to be bad with numbers or sloppy with details. The role was typically occupied by a seasoned E5, but my squadron believed I was up for the task. It was the perfect opportunity to prove myself as a quick student and a solid leader. I observed the officers and chiefs around me. Their attitude, candor, and approach to the job. If I saw something that could help me, I added it to my mental tool kit, and if I saw an example of what not to do, I added that to memory as well.

Life on the *Ike* was such a contrast to life at home. It felt so unnatural being away from my son. I hoped he would be too young to ever remember I was gone. One day I had a talk with CMC Washington about fatherhood and how his time in the navy affected the relationship he held with his son. I admired his service and the respect he received throughout the ship. Commander Master Chief Washington had been enlisted for twenty-five-plus years. I asked him plainly, "Has it all been worth it? Do you feel like you've been there for your son?" He seemed startled by my candidness. I had no reason to be shy, this topic was too personal. I was considering my options for life.

"Well, Hillman, if you're asking me if my son and I are as close as I would want us to be, I have to say no. I've spent a lot of time away. I take care of anything for him and my wife, his mother, but she's the one he goes to when he needs something. She's the one he's been able to grab, cry on, and vent to when he was frustrated. My career has been good, it's provided me with resources for my family . . . but I could have been a better father." CMC Washington looked me in my eyes and kept it real with me. I didn't like his answer, but I know he was being honest. I wanted a different story for my relationship with Robert . . . I want to be there guiding him through the tears, frustration, and triumph after struggle. I'm the hands-on dad who needs to be involved, that's the type of father Teo and I talked about becoming. CMC Washington is an incredible man in my eyes and he'd reached the top of the ranks. I had no interest in judging his life or relationship to his son, however I knew that wasn't the journey or relationship I wanted for Robert and me.

I read this book called *He-Motions* by T. D. Jakes. *Even Strong Men Struggle* was the subtitle and that stood out to me. I was excelling professionally but I knew I had a tendency to struggle emotionally. I would feel weak when I was unable to articulate what I felt inside or in moments when I felt hurt by someone. "Face the giants in your life, slay them, and move on. Do not be daunted by the mistakes and failures in your life. You can't be a success if you don't know who you are." Like many of the books I read, *He-Motions* centered in on having a clear identity of self. We all have giants in our life, challenges we have to overcome, but the task is to face them, endure through the process, and move on. I spent a lot of time thinking about the decisions that led me to the navy. Getting Sequoyah pregnant, leaving my parents' home prematurely, and performing poorly at NSU. I wondered how different life would be if I made other choices. All in an attempt to face, slay, and grow beyond the thinking that influenced me to create my circumstances.

I was ready to move on from those decisions with no regrets.

It was January 21, 2010, just two days after Robert's second birthday, that the *Ike* entered our area of theater after transiting the Suez Canal. Soon after, we would launch our combat sortie missions in support of OEF in Afghanistan. It felt like déjà vu. Planes, parts, and no days off.

The difference this time was the amount of port stops. We

were away for six months, and the entire crew was excited about those precious days of liberty every few weeks. Our first port of call was Jebel Ali, UAE, a city located about twenty miles from Dubai. It would be a much-needed taste of liberty as by that time we hadn't been off the boat in sixty-eight days. As usual on those trips, we would drink, eat, and take in the city. Back on the ship it was business as usual. Off days are always the perfect recharge most of us needed.

Then on a calm March morning, a normal day at sea turned into a disastrous emergency. A helicopter assigned to a squadron in our Air Wing crashed into the Arabian Sea. The helicopter was returning from a mission in Afghanistan and was about five miles from the *Ike*. Three of four crew members were rescued and brought to the ship. And for the next three days, the fourth sailor remained missing at sea. With every passing hour it was harder and harder to imagine anyone surviving those conditions. On the fourth day, they ended the search for the missing officer and official navy word declared him deceased. I thought about his family at home, his friends, college classmates . . . maybe he had a pet. In the next few days they all would be receiving word that he was not coming home. They would hear mention of how honorably he had served, how much his time was appreciated, and that he would want them to be strong. But they wouldn't be hearing from him anymore. From the moment they received the news there would be a void; there would be someone missing.

Some say, "You know what you signed up for." And in it, they're saying, "Hey, you volunteered to be in the military. You knew people would die." It is true, military or not, people die. But when I signed up for the navy, I did not know I would feel so close to death every waking moment. One mishap, a quick series of events, and that could be my family receiving the same news. And I wasn't the only one with these thoughts. The ship always carried a very stiff and tense atmosphere after something drastic happened. How should a person feel when someone they see every day dies? How should someone act when they are scared, uncomfortable, and feeling stressed out? People forced injury to get rest, they doubled up on prescriptions to fight pain, and everyone kept moving trying to convince the ones around them that things were okay. Death is intense, but this was war. Rarely did we consider the trauma associated with it. Instead, we prepared for the next flight schedule. We were taught that the mission must continue.

The highlight of most days was getting an email from my family and friends at home in Virginia. My boy Joey and a few others were still in college, partying, living it up every night. All they talked about was sports, girls, and turning up. I felt like we were worlds apart with our concerns day to day. When they asked, "How's life going?" I was thinking about radars, fuel budgets, and repair schedules but instead I would respond, "I can't complain, same ol' same ol'." Aside from conversations with my boys, I'd email with a few girls I knew to fill my void in the area of romance. It reminded me why I loved writing letters so much throughout my life. Organization is an important part of the job and I developed great indexing skills. I broke my emails up into categories, dividing them into favorites, frequent contacts, and any personal writings.

When I wasn't dreaming about the rest of my life, the next job, career path, and the opportunities I wanted to have, my thoughts would flow to some vision of Robert. I dreamed of how he was growing up and the different things he could be doing. What was he thinking about, and who was teaching him? Was he running, learning more words? I imagined it all.

To keep my thoughts balanced I decided to work on some professional qualifications. I studied to earn my pin as an aviation warfare specialist. I felt like a Boy Scout working for his next notch, doing busywork for ribbons and medals to show. The test was challenging and required a lot of studying. To pass there is a live interview with a panel of senior ranking members who ask all kinds of question to test your knowledge. I passed without missing a question and proudly donned my winged aviation warfare pin. I was ready for my next challenge.

SOC, an association of approximately nineteen hundred accredited colleges and universities, offers specific associate and bachelor's degrees to military members worldwide through resident courses or distance learning. Deployment, transfer orders, and work demands make it very difficult to complete a college degree. Colleges taking part in each curriculum area guarantee acceptance of each other's credits for transfer. In my off time on the *Ike* I took courses with Ashford University. All classes were recorded on our SMART transcript. These were official military transcripts which were used by colleges to validate our actual credited training. We received college-like credits for basic training, class A school, and different trainings we completed throughout our service. Every sailor had a SMART transcript created for them and access to it was free.

My first courses with Ashford were two of the ones I failed while attending NSU: College Algebra and English 102. I was in class with sailors of all ranks, from airmen to chiefs. It was unspoken but we all were there for a common reason. Navy careers don't last forever. Regardless of how decorated and seasoned a sailor becomes, there is a cap. A point where the job no longer needs you. College degrees signify passage into opportunity, another beginning, possibly into an area of your passion. For me, I was there to finish what I started my freshman year on campus.

The classroom atmosphere was serious and though the professors were civilian, we gave them the same courtesy and respect we offered officers. I found pockets of time within the day to get homework assignments and research papers done. It was important to be resourceful and diligent without getting distracted from my duties. If my college work began getting in the way of my navy tasks, I knew I wouldn't be allowed to finish the courses. But I never had any issues. I knew what needed to be done and made it happen.

June 7, 2010, the *Ike* pulled into Khalifa bin Salman Port at Hidd, Bahrain. I followed my routine from our visit the previous year. I stayed on base to Skype home and speak with my family. Robert was sleeping when I called but it was good to see the image of him on the screen resting. My mother's voice was so soothing to hear. I could feel the love flowing from her lips and saw in her eyes how much she wanted me to be home.

"Less than sixty days, Mom. You know I can't tell you the exact day we're pulling in, but we'll be home soon. I promise.

I love you and thank you for being the best grandma in the world!" I signed off Skype feeling blessed to have a good family back home. People who missed me and made sure I didn't have to worry about things going crazy in my absence.

Not everyone was so fortunate. At the table beside me, I overheard a sailor talking to what appeared to be his wife. "You cannot do this to me, you fucking bitch!" He slammed his computer shut and stormed out of the room fuming. With so many days at sea, I collected a vast memory bank of "Dear John" stories, I don't know where to start. Divorce . . . Cheating . . . Pregnant by the neighbor? Gambled all the money away? I heard horror story after horror story of romance going wrong. Oversharing happens by default at sea; I discovered five chiefs in my squadron alone were married to their third wives. They would joke, "You can't make chief until you have your second divorce." I never laughed. Relationships and marriage were no joke to me, but I was beginning to see that they were no match for the military. Time apart truly reveals the quality and substance of a relationship. We hope to have someone thinking about us and reaching out with goodness while we're away. Still we know in our hearts that any person reaching back would rather have us close, not on a ship, not somewhere on Skype, but there with them.

After six long months, it was time to head home. We spent July Fourth transiting the Suez Canal headed for the Mediterranean Sea. Our mission was successful and the entire ship was happy to be done with our final scheduled deployment.

July 6, 2010, the *Ike* arrived in Antalya, Turkey, for a three-day port visit. Frye and Gray were both up to transfer commands when we returned home. We decided any ports from here until Norfolk would be spent celebrating our sea fellowship and the brotherhood we created. I bought the first round of drinks, Frye the next, Gray the third, and we repeated the cycle again. We talked about family—Frye was happily married, Gray started the cruise happily married but he wasn't going home that way, and I was the single young guy taking in all their perspective. After our drinks we walked the streets of the old city, wrapping around a Roman-era harbor. For dinner we picked a cliff-top restaurant with views of the hazy blue mountain silhouettes. It was a celebration worth raising a toast to. I was no stranger to goodbyes, but I knew I was going to miss having these guys by my side.

While I was deployed I did not maintain much communication with my dad Dana. I assumed he didn't have an email address and he was always clear about not being text savvy. Our communication on deployments reminded me of how rarely we spoke when I was younger as we moved farther away from him to different locations. I held a stern, "I'll talk to you when I get back" disposition. He never complained so I assumed it worked for both of us.

I read many books throughout the months at sea to gain wisdom. I loaded up my order cart on Amazon with different books to be shipped to us on the *Ike*. Authors like Norman Vincent Peale, Julia Cameron, Matthew Kelly, Marianne Williamson, Brené Brown, James Baldwin, Iyanla Vanzant, Zadie Smith, Zora Neale Hurston, and so many more. I wanted to soak up as much wisdom and information as possible. I knew growing in awareness, knowledge, and through other people's stories that I had a chance of becoming a better writer. It felt like I was putting myself through a mini university experience. What started as a journey to challenge myself to be an avid reader began to be something that made my spirit feel better. With each book I read, the more I was inspired to write down more of my own thoughts, beliefs, and experiences to share with others.

One early morning a remarkably vivid dream woke me up before my alarm sounded. In the dream I was much older, my son looked to be about sixteen. I walked into the room to see him at his desk reading a book and giving it his full attention. I walked closer, he looked up and smiled briefly but lowered his head and continued to read. Just as I was within feet of him I recognized the name on the cover of the book. It was my name, in bold letters across the top. With a sudden rush of excitement, I thought, *Wow! My son is reading my book.* He looked so much like me at his age, sitting there taking notes in his journal. At sixteen, I was obsessed with finishing a good book whenever I found one. I always wrote down the sentences that stood out to me. I woke up exhilarated. It feels so good to remember a positive dream. *I'll be an author one day*, I mused as I dressed to go to the gym. Though that day wasn't happening in the foreseeable future while I was deployed on the ship, I at least wanted to hold on to the thought. I knew my dream meant something.

Making your mark as a sailor is much different than validating yourself as a father. Raising a person feels unlike any other job; it's the most emotional relationship for me. Deployment is hard on everyone, and being away made me feel like an absent father. I would remind myself that I did not leave him, that I was only away on a work trip so that I could come back and provide what he needed. I knew in a few days we would be home, and I was prepared to earn Robert's love and trust. At his age he wouldn't be able to ask where I was the last few months; he was only two. There was no speech I needed to prepare to prove my worth to him as his father. Now that I was home, I just had to be there for him, right there by his side. "The closer I am, the stronger we'll be."

After reunion comes reintegration, and while both are exciting, reintegration is harder than it looks. Sailors come home exhausted, anxious, jet-lagged, emotionally overwhelmed, and quite possibly with a huge to-do list from work. It's helpful if you have an understanding family because they aren't looking to dump all your duties back on you the second you walk into the house. Still, everyone knew I was back. And the women in my family joked that it was "time for the navy to share." I wasn't the first man they covered for on deployment, it's kind of tradition for them now. My GeGe looked over my mother and her sisters while Papa deployed. My mom looked over my sisters and me anytime my dad Frank deployed. And my entire family looked over my son while I deployed. I came back ready to show my full appreciation.

To be away for an extended period of time changes both you and your support system. Sequoyah and I would only speak on rare occasions while I was away. I could tell we were both entering new phases of our lives and that our romantic relationship was dead. We had some arguments about initial arrangements for Robert's day-care provider but nothing boiled over into any-thing major. I was warned that the shock of change may go hand in hand with some resentment. I didn't want to open up and let her see how I was evolving, and it didn't appear that she wanted me to see any new sides of her. I can see some resentment in that, but it's more accurate to say that we had no interest in being close friends. I was away, she was in Virginia with Robert. We both had our own challenges but regardless of the challenge, someone always thinks the other had it easier. In our case, she wasn't the one working a nonstop flight schedule in the Arabian Sea for thirteen of the last twenty-four months. And I wasn't the one solo parenting without a partner, depending on the support of my deployed baby daddy's family. Neither of us had the ideal situation. Life isn't always ideal.

I was no longer physically working on the ship, but I was still employed by the navy. At work some of us would talk about how it felt to finally be home. I'd see some guys coming in early just to get away from the house, others asking to stand duty, and some looking up legal advice. Cars got towed for expired tags, some sailors' homes got robbed while away. "I feel like a damn stranger in my own house . . . like I'm tiptoeing around every-body. How do I pay the mortgage but I'm in the fucking way? I'd rather be here," I heard one sailor admit. For some, it can be a rather haywire environment because work doesn't stop for their personal issues.

Long deployments can take a toll on a person. But for every person battling problems with money, communication, or re-lationship and trust issues, there are also sailors experiencing positive reintegration with their family.

With me, I struggled with being intimate. I had no intentions of being vulnerable with anyone about "what happened on deployment" because there was nothing to talk about. I made small talk about the work and ports, and diverted conversations to anything that wasn't navy affiliated. All that time away and the many significant things that happened during it, I would feel selfish trying to download that on to a person. And I did not want any pity, I just wanted life to move forward. But holding back made the intimacy I had been longing to feel seem even further away. I think my friends and family expected me to be the same Robert I always was, and some of my boys would joke about me being so serious.

I held things in. War is often an ugly business with many innocent victims. I knew I assisted in bombs and bullets being dropped, lives being taken. I heard tapes of pilot missions, even saw video of targets being destroyed. The experience of war isn't something I wanted to talk about. My dad Frank never talked about his time in Desert Storm, Kuwait, or Iraq, and he commanded artillery divisions. It wasn't until I myself served that I gained the full scope of his possible combat duties. What we all experience, combat or not, is an extremely long period where we are absent from comfort, security, our families, and breaks.

On deployment, we tend to deal with one another in ways that are not normal in civilian America. We are harsh, we talk shit, we yell, and don't often act with kindness and gentleness toward one another. Each day sailors seemed suspicious, tightly wound, and easily angered. Sleeping is not easy and rest is limited, and even after a few months of being home from deployment, adjusting can still be difficult. One night, ambulance sirens woke me up in a panic, I jumped out of bed thinking it was a man-overboard drill. For a long phase I tried to adjust to having my life back. Old routines, usual route to work, and football Sundays with the family. It wasn't the same as before I left, and some days I just didn't want to leave the house. After coming home from the first one, I thought this time would be a piece of cake. But no, much like every other time I went away, life changed. I changed. And so did all the people whom I cared about. While away I wrote, "All good things grow differently." Reintegrating at home was proof. I saw how everyone matures naturally, especially when we had to be independent of one another. However, I was now home hoping to once again be present in the lives of my family and friends.

Settling in at home meant learning a new routine. My cousin Tori and I decided to get a bigger place, we also invited my friend Zach from NSU to be a roommate. I loved living in Holly Point and with the three of us, the house always had plenty going on. We loved to host people for different events. Tori and Zach were great support with Robert, especially when I had to stay overnight to stand duty at work. After work, when I picked him up from day care, I would walk Robert to the neighborhood park. The swings and slide were his favorite, but he lit up the most when I chased him around the sandbox. "Can't catch me," Robert would say in his young toddler voice. "Oh, yes I can, here I come. You better run, Rob." He would take off running as fast as he could and then he would stop and look back to see how close I was, whenever he saw me gaining on him, he raised his arms and said "Pick me up, Daddy! Pick me up!" I would spin him in the air and we repeated the game until I convinced him I knew something else fun.

These moments were all the validation I needed.

CHAPTER SEVEN

Nothing Is Going to Come Easy

On the work front, I was awarded Junior Sailor of the Quarter. An honor only given out four times a year per command in the navy. It was a good bullet on my evaluation to even be nominated as one of the four candidates for the annual award. Despite not winning Junior Sailor of the Year, I received another "Early Promote" evaluation. Going from Sailor of the Quarter to Sailor of the Year would have been a huge accomplishment, but it wasn't for me. This evaluation said enough. And with it, I confidently studied for my next advancement exam.

Before the end of the year the news came back that I passed the test for petty officer second class. I advanced to the rate/rank of LS2. Typically, it would have taken me five to eight years to reach this point and a more seasoned E5 let me know it. "Don't take it for granted, Hillman. I didn't make second class until I was seven years in. Now they're pushing guys like me out." Though the navy wasn't in my retirement plan, I heard him loud and clear.

The time for taking the blessings of life for granted was behind me. This promotion reflected the internal growth that I was working hard to manifest, and for me it was a great sign that I was proving my worth.

Co-Parenting Woes

I imagine most fathers want to be actively involved with their children. Even fathers like me, who no longer have an intimate relationship with their child's mother, still want to be a parent. We want a quality relationship with our child and to be able to spend time with them. Unfortunately, some mothers and fathers are unable to find common ground on important issues when it comes to co-parenting. So in every US state there are several family and domestic courts that attempt to help solve the problems that parents are unable to work through together. Many fathers don't understand their rights where children are concerned and unfortunately, their rights are sometimes overlooked throughout the court process.

Here are some examples of "Father's Rights":

To spend time with his children
To be involved in his children's lives

To have equal participation in parenting, including where
    they live, go to school, and attend church
To have equal access to medical and school records
To have equal say in medical decisions
To have the ability to parent or discipline his children
    without interference from their mother

Sequoyah and I were trying to co-parent to the best of our
ability. We had successfully come to an agreement on Robert
Jr.'s surgery. He was developing on pace. He could walk, laugh,
talk, feed himself, and was learning to use the bathroom on
his own. Another thing that I thought we had come to terms
on was how we'd split custody of Robert. My week with him
started on Sunday afternoon. We switched at two p.m. the following Sunday and then she had him for seven days until the
next Sunday came and we switched again. We rarely engaged in
much conversation if it wasn't directly concerning our son. So
no, there was no stressing each other out every day. Robert was
fortunate: both of his parents still called Chesapeake home and
lived within fifteen miles of each other. But when it was time to
switch day-care providers, Sequoyah and I seemed to be worlds
apart. I liked our current arrangement. Robert was comfortable
with his routine, and if there were any problems at day care my
mom could help—she lived five minutes away. The trip was less
convenient for Sequoyah, who had moved in with her mom and
wanted to pick a provider that was closer to their house.

A couple days after our small disagreement about little Rob's
day-care situation, and which one was the best to go with, Sequoyah informed me that she was filing for custody of Robert.

"We'll let the judge decide," she said in a text message. In the early stages of her pregnancy we had many talks about avoiding the family court process at all costs. I didn't think we needed a judge telling us when and how to raise our son. But Sequoyah was done talking things out with me. And reading the text from her made me angry. I was terrified of going to court and losing Robert. From the experiences I heard my shipmates explain, juvenile and domestic court was an expensive and invasive process, and it usually doesn't fare in the favor of fathers. I didn't want any mention of me being in jail in the past to come back up and hinder me from presenting a fair case for myself as a good parent for Robert.

In order to establish rights, a parent has to file a petition through their local courthouse. This petition works as a request for the court to begin initial processing of custody and legal rights for the child. I wasn't sure exactly when Sequoyah filed her petition but I knew I wanted whoever would be looking at it to see that I was following suit. I filed for joint physical and legal custody of Robert to maintain the arrangement we currently had. Outside of our day-care dispute, I didn't know Sequoyah's full motivation for filing. Part of me wanted to ask her "why?" but I never acted on the impulse.

A few weeks later I received mail from the Virginia Department of Social Services. I opened the envelope to see child support paperwork. These are court ordered payments to support your child, usually made by the noncustodial parent. I folded the papers as I got up from my bed. I was angry again, but not enough to disrupt Robert's afternoon nap. I went into the bathroom and sat on the floor across from the toilet. I tried to breathe, but I felt suffocated. The tears in my eyes started to well. I associated two things with child support: being broke forever and jail. I wanted nothing to do with either option.

In Virginia, laws don't favor either parent, but instead compare the relationship of each parent with the child to determine custody and visitation. When a father or mother wants equal access to parent his or her child, then they must also equally share in all the responsibilities of raising the child, including financial support. The problem most fathers in cases like mine face is that mothers don't seem to have to worry about losing any of their rights. My mother was awarded full custody of my sister and me without contest from my dad Dana. My dad Frank's ex-wife had full custody of my brother, Frankie. My aunt Daiquiri had full custody of my cousins Tori and Jewell. This wasn't something only limited to my family. It's no secret that mothers are consistently more likely to win full custody of the children.

I still had to take my chances. If the courts deemed Sequoyah to be the better parent for Robert by their standards, I would disagree, but I would be willing to accept it. A few days went by and I received another letter which informed me that the first recommendation of the court in our custody case was a mediation session with Sequoyah and me. The two of us met with a woman in Chesapeake a few miles from the courthouse. She began by stating that she was not a judge and had no final say in our case. She made it clear that her presence was only to gain more information on our issues and possibly steer us toward a peaceful resolution. The mediator asked us a series of questions about what we believed was best for our son, Robert.

"Which one of you do you think will provide the best
   quality of life for Robert?"
"Which one of you is financially prepared to support
   raising him alone?"
"What are your current living arrangements?"
"Have either one of you graduated college?"

Question after question, but neither Sequoyah nor I budged.
We both believed we were the best parent for Robert and neither of us saw any room for giving in. We left the mediation
session with our issues unresolved. I appreciated the mediator
asking some serious questions, but I had little faith in our problems being fixed during a random thirty-minute powwow with
a stranger.

   "Meeting tonight at the IHOP in Greenbrier at eight p.m.
Sequoyah and her mom will be there too." I called my mother
right after I read her text.

   "Mom, what's going on?" I inquired with urgency.

   "Well, as Robert's grandmothers, Cristel and I decided to
solve this custody thing for you two. Why don't you come over
the house beforehand so we can talk about it? We have to meet
them in two hours," she said with her motherly "Just trust me"
tone. When I arrived at my parents' house I was met by my
smiling mother at the door, and in her hands, she held a typed
agreement. "Sit down and read this, then let's talk."

   I followed her instructions and read the papers carefully. "The
Grandmas'" proposed custody arrangement mapped out an equal
plan for Robert. The two of us would both keep two weeks out of
the month, rotating on Sunday. Sequoyah was given first prefer-

ence on day-care arrangements and we would revisit terms when it came time to choose a school for kindergarten. On even years I was to claim Robert on my taxes and on the odd years she would file claiming him as a dependent. There would be no child support or restricting any parent or grandparent from free and open access to Robert at any time. His medical and dental insurance would continue being covered under my navy policy.

After reading the document I could only marvel at how resourceful my mother always proved to be. I watched her repair computers, cook unforgettable meals, and now I was watching her be my legal aid. We left the house and made it to IHOP with ten minutes to spare. I informed the hostess of our party size and Sequoyah and her mom pulled up a few moments later. We were seated at the table across from each other, facing off with our mothers beside us. The situation felt silly, but the tone was fitting for the way Sequoyah and I were acting with each other. We were the young, inexperienced parents with no patience. Our mothers carried the role of seasoned veterans who knew we could handle our problems without hurting our son in the process. Still, neither of us talked directly to each other. We played the whole thing out as if we were adults stuck with our eighth grade mentality.

"Listen, the only person that gets hurt here is little Robert. Get over yourself and think about your son. He needs both of his parents in his life," my mom preached.

"That's right. The two of you don't have to go to court to work this out. This agreement is good. My grandson can come stay with his Granny if y'all keep acting crazy," Cristel said keeping a straight face.

Our attitudes didn't stop our mothers from being diligent and making sure we both agreed to sign the agreement right there at the table. We both signed two copies. Before getting up from the table, The Grandmas made us verbally agree to be the best parents that we could be for Robert. Obediently, we granted their request.

The next day I was eager to take the agreement to the court. Our mediator informed us that as parents we could establish our own custody and visitation agreement before our first court date. Once we had a written arrangement signed by both parties, it can then be filed with the court to serve as an official order. I was relieved and hopeful Sequoyah and I would never have to revisit the custody process ever again. Walking out of the courtroom that afternoon was one of the happiest days of my life.

Creating an Audience

At work, I enjoyed the new casual pace within our command. Now that deployment was behind us, everyone seemed to be focused on finding out what duty assignment the navy was sending them to next. I had less than one year left in my enlistment, and I planned to take as much time as possible weighing my options.

Every morning after our maintenance meeting I would take a trip up to the "officers'" restroom. I'd go partly because my body can't handle coffee and greasy breakfast sandwiches, but mostly I went to get some thinking done. I won't spend much time creating that visual for you, but I spent a great deal of time writing on the toilet in the bathroom stall. The officers' restroom attracted less visitors, always had fresh toilet paper, and I could be alone. Whether I actually had to use the restroom or not, I would still sit there for twenty minutes each morning drafting a message I called "Thoughts for the Day" (TFTD). The stall was my personal think station. I typed each message in the notes app of my BlackBerry cell phone then transferred the final copy to the email on my laptop. It was a seamless process for me.

When I first began writing the TFTD messages, I only wanted to share them with the family and friends on my email list. I started the small group with twenty-two people in 2009 and they were the ones who kept my inbox full with conversation, jokes, and pictures while I was deployed. Since then, in its two-year existence, my TFTD email group had grown ten times its initial size.

"Hey Rob, I just want to say I love your morning emails. My coworker usually forwards them to me, but she's no longer working here. I was wondering if you could add me? I promise to forward them to our department just like she did." I smiled reading the email. I loved to see the list grow organically, by people reaching out, and not because I was stealing email addresses and spamming inboxes.

After emailing the TFTD to my list of contacts I would break the message up to fit the 140-character Twitter limit. At nine thirty each morning I would send the TFTD message into the Twitter atmosphere for whoever was willing to read it. I had more contacts in my email than followers but Twitter offered a more immediate response to my words. My profile was public and open for anyone to view, and I enjoyed analyzing the dialogue my TFTD content was attracting in addition to my email list. I started setting goals for growing my audience. I wanted one new Twitter follower, or one new email subscriber every day, which would indicate to me that there was one more person in the world who might be affirmed by my words. I was inspired to write consistently, and was reminded of the enthusiasm I had during my initial studies at NSU.

I pushed myself to be the best writer that I could be. I wanted to write about things that people could relate to, with messages that helped people grow and learn. My motivation to write increased my appetite to read and learn as much as I could from other authors. During the first six months of 2011, I read numerous books, reading things concerning spirituality, cultural identity, trust, love, and intimacy. I was a sponge for information and wanted to be known as a resource for positivity and guidance. My favorite books during this time were:

- *The Assignment: Powerful Secrets for Discovering Your Destiny* by Mike Murdock
  "You will only be remembered for two things: the problems you solve or the ones you create."
- *The Purpose Driven Life: What on Earth Am I Here For?* by Rick Warren
  "The greatest gift you can give someone is your time."
- *The Alchemist* by Paulo Coelho
  "When we love, we always strive to become better than we are. When we strive to become better than we are, everything around us becomes better too."
- *Intimacy: Trusting Oneself and the Other* by Osho

"Once you are incapable of loving yourself, you will never be able to love anybody. That is an absolute truth, there are no exceptions to it. You can love others only if you are able to love yourself."

- *I May Not Get There with You: The True Martin Luther King, Jr.* by Michael Eric Dyson
". . . what became problematic was King's insistence that merit, not race, should determine how education and employment are distributed."
- *Holler If You Hear Me: Searching for Tupac Shakur* by Michael Eric Dyson
"I think I'm a natural-born leader. I know how to bow down to authority if it's authority that I respect."
- *Why I Love Black Women* by Michael Eric Dyson
"When we love black women, we love ourselves, and the God who made us."

I spent more time reading during this period than any other time in my life. The more I read, the more confident I felt with my own voice as a writer. On one occasion I received an email from someone in my TFTD group asking how I was able to write new material so consistently. The person expressed being an aspiring writer and frustrated by the discomfort they faced with writer's block. I knew the feeling all too well, throughout the years I had many periods where I was unable to create new original work or write anything I thought was meaningful. After reflecting on the best response possible, I offered the quote that helps me break through the barriers of writer's block:

"When you sit down to write, write. Don't do anything else except go to the bathroom."

—STEPHEN KING

Challenges at Work

I am a United States Sailor.
I will support and defend the Constitution of the United States of America and I will obey the orders of those appointed over me.
I represent the fighting spirit of the Navy and those who have gone before me to defend freedom and democracy around the world.
I proudly serve my country's Navy combat team with Honor, Courage, and Commitment.
I am committed to excellence and the fair treatment of all.

—THE SAILOR'S CREED

We learn it as early as basic training and we promise to stand by it throughout our time of service.

Robert Jr. was only four months when I joined the navy. And by the time he reached school age I wanted a plan in place to leave the navy. My fear in staying was that I would miss the more important moments of his young life, and that my absence is what he would remember about me. I wanted to be a full-time and fully engaged father. Whether it was doing homework, surprising the class with snacks, or going on field trips, I wanted to be there whenever Robert needed me.

For fathers and mothers that work full- or part-time, go to school, or even just need a break from the pressures of parenting, finding affordable, quality childcare is more than just important, it is absolutely necessary. For sailors, we generally get two options: the on-base childcare center which typically has a long wait list or is slow with their placement. Or work it out yourself. I chose the latter. My entire family lived within twenty miles of one another, and served as a great support system. I never had any issues with finding childcare, and the navy never made any complaints.

However, some things were beginning to feel very different within our command at the squadron. As people transferred out and roles were replaced with new faces, our slower-paced work environment began to feel more like a political game. I felt like that kid at school watching all his friends graduate and move on to a better place without me. And the newcomers wanted to make their mark on the new territory; they wanted to impress the teachers and the principal. I understood, before them I was the newcomer eager to prove my worth. Ready to impress the maintenance officer, Frye, and CMC Washington. But all of those people were gone now and it was clear that there would be changes.

I was assigned to rotate to night check supervisor instead of my normal role as Financial Operations Manager and assistant day check supervisor. The new leading petty officer (LPO) within my division decided it was time to groom a different sailor for the position. The role as night check supervisor was made to be like a promotion of some sort. But I knew I wasn't a favorite for the new boss and he wanted somebody else to receive the recognition my role garnered. I trained my new apprentice but I wanted a promise from my chief and LPO that "night check supervisor" would be only temporary. I was okay with not having to work beside either of them for a few weeks, but in the long run I knew the night check work hours would present a major problem for me. My chief and LPO both said, "LS2, in the navy we have a mission first, family second motto. All sailors must be available to work all hours. I can't make any promises."

I fought the decision by taking my grievance above my chief's and LPO's pay grade. I never agreed with the "mission first, family second" motto that many of my shipmates accepted. I wasn't planning to be that chief with three marriages or that sailor who wasn't close to their child. I wrote this letter to the commanding officer of my squadron, our highest-ranking officer and the final decision maker.

20 AUGUST 2011
Dear Commander Hewlett,

Upon checking into the command I was informed that new sailors who are single and have dependents are required to have a family caregiver plan on file. This plan had to be approved and agreed upon by three parties—the service member, the caregiver, and the final approval of the squadron's Commanding Officer. I was informed that the plan had normal working hours and that mine would be from 0600–1600, this is included on the current plan in my service record, and signed in agreement by all required parties.

It would be absurd for me to act as if I'm the only single parent in the military and I am not using my son as a crutch. However, my support system cannot bear the weight of me working night check indefinitely for our squadron. There is no consistency in the hours and time of relief. This would require me to disturb my parents' house at 3AM every night and they are not supporting this option.

Example scenario would be me going into work at 1430 and paying somebody to watch my son at night, and we already pay for daycare—his mom works too. Getting off work anywhere between 0130 and 0230, picking up my 3 year old from my parents' house at 0300, and then us getting home by 0330–0345. He is a young child, he doesn't operate on "night hours" or a flight schedule. He's awake and ready for his day at 7AM, I would have no time to sleep and no energy to interact with him. Additionally, I do not have the funds required to pay for day and night care.

I understand the command is requiring me to work night check hours and that being on sea duty mandates that I have the appropriate caregiver plan on file to cover me for whatever shift is required. The current caregiver plan I have covers me to work a full day shift and for my first two years in the squadron it has worked out without any issues. Granted we have been deployed or working extended hours preparing for deployment 18 of those 24 *months. My evaluations will speak to the quality of my service, I am committed to the work we do but I am being forthright about the limitations I have. Working night shift creates a lot of problems for my support system and I . . .*

I have proven to the command and the Navy that I was deployable and fully capable of getting the mission done at the highest tempo. All I'm asking for is some compassion for my situation and some empathy in its regard. I'm one of the few parents in my division, the only government purchase card holder, and the sailors with no dependents have offered to work nights.

I've missed a great deal of time as far as the day-to-day parenting duties with my son these first two years of his life. Now that we aren't deploying for a while my support system expects me to be the father I recognize myself as. As a parent it is my duty not only to provide financially but with time as well. I have to be there and present. My support system has helped me beyond measure getting through these hard times. I appreciate all the command has done for me and its continued support of my role as a sailor and my role as a father. Thank you for your time.

Sincerely,
LS2(AW) Robert Hillman

The conflict with my work schedule coupled with wanting to spend more time with Robert made it feel like the walls were closing in on me. I was fighting Sequoyah for my time with Robert and now I was battling my superiors for it. After I submitted the letter, I never received an official response from our CO, but the next week my chief and LPO rotated me back to day check to assume my normal duties. Nobody ever mentioned night check to me again.

I Want My Own Book

I got my own, roommate-free apartment in Virginia Beach during the summer of 2011. It was a one-bedroom, one-bath place, no bigger than nine hundred square feet off of Level Green Road. I bought my first desk and office chair. I assembled them as if they were the final tools I needed to accomplish my goal of becoming a published author. This was my writing station and I wanted nothing else to happen in this space but writing. There was a window to my right that overlooked the trees and a pool area. Behind me, I set up a mini basketball hoop for Robert to use while keeping me company in the room. He liked to be close and within sight, so on my breaks I would turn around and play with him. We had a good flow going and he didn't interrupt my writing. When I got up from my desk to take breaks, Robert would put his wrestling figurines, the basketball, and whatever else down to take a break with me. When I returned to my writing station, he went back to playtime.

In front of my desk there was a corkboard, dry-erase board, and a calendar. I hung each one on the wall side by side. I placed notes, inspirational pictures, and dates for writing deadlines on them. I painted the center wall of my living room red and bought some candles to accompany my desk. I wanted the right ambience to assist me in paying attention to detail and staying focused. So far, I'd amassed well over three hundred TFTD messages and I used them as inspiration to begin building an outline for my book. But I struggled to find a title for the book.

It'll just come to me.

When I was in college at NSU, I got into blogging. I created my first platform on a website titled Blogspot.com. The process was fairly simple. You sign up, choose a name for your blog, a theme, with color and border options, and then you're done. You can start adding content from there. It was a free service. For my blog, I chose the name "About Something Real." I had thought long and hard about the meaning, and what people would interpret from it. I wanted to play on our social concept of "what's real" in love, relationships, and life. My blog housed poems, journal entries, one-sentence thoughts, and color schemes that didn't always mesh well together. My computer design skills weren't to be desired. And the blog did not receive much traffic.

My TFTD email group didn't require any graphics or have any weblinks. It was simple: I write, send it, and the readers that had something to say would respond. I enjoyed the feedback, and the deeply personal stories readers would share with me triggered by my own thoughts. It felt connective, like even though I was still trying to figure out my life, I knew I wasn't alone. "You should write a book," became the most consistent comment. It felt good. No, it felt great. It felt like I mattered. It gave me a purpose.

Family Investments

September 17, 2011

My mom planned a surprise party for my twenty-fourth birthday. I walked into my parents' house to see most of my immediate family in attendance. Grandparents, aunts, cousins, sisters, and my boys. I was asked to stop at the door, to stand there and to just listen as they celebrated me for my birthday. One by one, each person pulled a piece of paper from behind their back. I could not tell what was on the papers but I assumed that maybe they wrote me an original song or something. Instead, one by one, my mom, Papa, GeGe, Frank, Elise, Joey, Miran, Latoria, Jewell, Aunt Daiquiri, and Aunt Derricka all read to me. The words on the papers in their hands were mine from my "Thoughts for the Day" series.

Once everyone was done reading, my mom announced that there was another surprise for me. "Stand right there, hold your hands out, and close your eyes," she said emphatically. I stood there, eyes closed, hands out, with my palms ready to hold whatever was coming. After placing the rectangular box in my hand, my mom said, "Okay, now you can open your eyes and open the box." I glanced up from looking at the box to observe the smiling faces reflecting on my family and friends. I could see anticipation and excitement in their eyes.

I slowly opened the box and there it was, my face on the cover of an actual book. My book, with its black background and bold gray and red lettering. I had been dreaming, planning, and thinking of a concept for my first book but here it was right in my hands. The title: *About Something Real*. I found it appropriate that the first blog I ever named was now the title of my first book.

About Something Real is a compilation of my TFTD pieces, 153 pages of my opinions and beliefs at the time. The cover was designed by my friend Zach, and my parents paid for five hundred copies to be printed. My mom formatted the book herself. One week later I was preparing for my first book signing.

I also now needed to figure out a plan to sell those books to the people who were familiar with my work. I had two starting points: my email list and social media. I knew before I could announce my book to either audience, I had to have some sort of website for them to view. I started searching the Internet for a place to build a website fast. GoDaddy had this "website tonight" feature, where you could customize and build a basic home page to host your product. I signed up for a PayPal account to handle the transactions and made sure we had the capabilities to ship globally.

My first book signing was a success. My family and friends were there and it felt tremendous being recognized by the people closest to me as a published author. They were proud and I felt surrounded by love and support. But things moved slowly after the initial excitement of release. Copies of *About Something Real* weren't exactly flying out of my trunk. There were months that went by without a single sale, and others where I was able to generate a few online orders and some face-to-face interest. My first two international sales came from Twitter followers. If I was not there to mail them myself, I would not have believed anyone telling me my books were traveling to Nairobi and Johannesburg. I'd dreamed of visiting these places since I was a child.

As the winter months came and 2012 approached, I knew final decision time was coming. I had two choices: stay or leave. Sailor or civilian. The options were clear, but making the choice wasn't so simple. I had less than five months left to figure out the answer to the question I had been asking myself since my early conversations with CMC Washington, Frye, and other sailors who had enough navy time to retire . . . "Is this really the best thing for me?"

"You can go, Hillman, just be back here in time for duty Monday morning." My chief wasn't exactly thrilled to approve my request, but for some reason, he did anyway. A milestone was in front of me: I booked my first paid public speaking event. Clemson University's chapter of Alpha Kappa Alpha sorority invited me to join them on campus in South Carolina for their Founder's Day celebration in January. But I still needed permission from my chain of command to attend or take leave. All activity that is outside of a one-hundred-mile radius of the base has to be pre-approved. The distance from Chesapeake, Virginia, to Clemson, South Carolina, is roughly 456 miles, and takes about an eight-hour drive. After getting approval, Elise and I rented a car, booked a hotel room at a Courtyard Marriott, and got on the road.

The morning of the speech I was nervous, excited, and all the other emotions that cause butterflies to stir in your stomach. I had very little experience speaking in front of an audience. I just wanted it to go well. The plan: "Tell your truth." So I talked about my experiences in college and the perils of misusing my time. I talked about planning and patience, revisiting my nights in jail and the months on the *Ike*. I talked about moving around throughout my childhood and the spiritual woes that come from blocking people out and refusing to forgive. I talked for well over an hour to a room of less than thirty people, and damn did it feel good to be heard. My transparency and honesty were well received. I ended my speech to the sound of applause, smiles, and even tears from some in the room. I left Clemson that day feeling a greater sense to grow and examine the meaning of my life. If there was anything within me or my experiences that could help someone else get over a hurdle, beyond a challenge, or accept some genuine love, I wanted to use it.

On the following Monday morning, I planned to be the first one in the office. When I arrived, I sat at my desk to see new orders waiting. The navy was preparing the next stop for me. As I opened the orders I remember a nervous feeling brewing inside. The Office of Naval Intelligence—Suitland, Maryland. This was a big opportunity and complete shift from the sea duty life I'd grown accustomed to in my squadron. Shore duty is supposed to be different, no deployments, a set work schedule, and an easy workload. The position also came with a top secret security clearance, higher assistance for housing, and a chance for promotion to E6. Again, a big opportunity, one with potential for high visibility among the fleet's most powerful officers.

I could even dust off that STA-21 application and revisit my officer candidacy.

But living in Suitland meant living away from Robert. I didn't want to be one hour away in Richmond when I considered transferring schools, so how would four hours away work? That would be tough. Fighting to make sure he was comfortable again when I walked off for deployments was traumatic for me. Every time I thought about moving, I followed those thoughts with the fear of leaving Robert and losing our closeness. And I did not consider taking him with me because I didn't want to fight Sequoyah. We'd just settled and I wanted peace between us.

"So what are you going to do now?" my career counselor asked me in our meeting about my separation. The command sets up these mandatory meetings so we are aware of our options. The only option I was interested in was separation.

"I'm an author now. I'm going back to school and I'll write books full-time. I just want to work for myself and be a father."

"An author? You know print media is dying right, LS2 Hillman? Everything is digital, nobody is reading books anymore. And if they are, the books aren't from unknown authors who don't even have a degree. Now, listen, I know you're ambitious and you want to go out there and show the world what you can do. I understand that you already put one book out and you're really excited to do more but maybe you should stay in, complete your degree while making some money to support you and your son. I mean how much do you expect to make on your own? What type of insurance will you have? If you don't come up with a better plan you'll be back in a year."

I felt unsupported in my decision. It angered me and hurt all at once. Before I joined the navy, I did not think of it as a place that showed people how much they were capable of accomplishing in the world. But that's exactly what my time in the service showed me. I became a better individual after learning to become a good sailor. Venturing out on the high seas and leaving family behind required me to deepen my faith and trust in God. It's what sparked my mission to become an author and speaker. But, the whole plan felt cheap when other people would repeat the titles to me. "From sailor to author and public speaker, huh?" They'd ask for clarification. Like I was leaving a sure thing for a pipe dream. Many of my fellow sailors seemed to have this "without the navy I can't make it in life" mind-set, as if that was the best it was going to be for them and since I was already in, it must be the best for me too. I'd be talking about pursuing my career as an author and I'd get looks that suggested I was throwing my life away.

"With all the time I give to the navy, if I used that same time working for myself building my own company and product, I could make my dreams come true," I explained to my mom. I was hoping she would agree, or at least help me vet my options. Instead, she just listened patiently. I took it as a sign that my plan wasn't convincing enough. So I talked more.

"I just want to enjoy what I do for a living, Mom. To wake up happy about what's going to happen for the next ten hours." I continued: "The biggest lesson I learned about myself in the navy, you know what that is, Mom?" She nodded, knowing I was going to tell her anyway. "The biggest lesson I learned in the navy is that I can be good—even at the things that I hate. The task can be hard, confusing, and arduous but I can still be good at it." I caught myself trying to convince her. But the more I spoke, the more I was convincing myself.

My mom's advice was to "Consider all options and make the best decision for your family."

I thought long and hard about the benefits of entrepreneurship. The freedom in making your own schedule intrigued me the most. That meant unlimited time with my son, no missing out on important moments, and no more asking for permission to be there for him. Whatever job gave me that comfort is the one I wanted most.

With leaving the navy there were also consequences to consider. I could no longer expect to receive automatic payments on the first and fifteenth of the month. No more free medical and dental benefits. No more thirty paid vacation days per year . . .

Ultimately, having flexibility outweighed everything else to me. If I became a civilian, I would figure out how to make money. I knew that about myself. I also liked the idea of being able to write as much as I wanted to, whenever I wanted to. I could be a real father, present in every way. That's my dream life.

JOURNAL ENTRY

Not everybody will see your vision or understand why you love what you love. We get so caught up in wanting people to see life through our lens. We want them to get why we want the things we want. We want that approval that we're doing the right thing. We can't make people believe in the mission, but we can have faith in ourselves and let our work speak for us. My plan B is just another way to make plan A work.

My active duty enlistment in the United States Navy ended on April 22, 2012. I woke up excited and filled with hope. This was the beginning of my new life, a new world where things happened on my time and according to my direction. I was officially a full-time writer and entrepreneur. And I knew nothing was going to come easy.

CHAPTER EIGHT

The Value of Consistency

Rejection and It Hurt Like Hell

Robert, I have something to tell you . . ."

I was only awake a few moments before my phone rang. It was my girlfriend, Slim. Our relationship was still new and just approaching the three-month mark. We spent a lot of time talking over the phone while getting to know each other, and I always looked forward to our conversations. This morning was no different, I was happy to hear her voice. She lived and worked four hours south of me in North Carolina, and was away in Chicago on a trip with some colleagues.

"What's going on?" I responded.

"Me and Ralph had sex last night . . ." I could hear Slim crying as she talked but I was stuck on those first few words. And a bit stunned.

"Slim, I appreciate you calling and telling me. I'm going to need a bit to think and process. Enjoy the rest of your trip." And I hung up the phone.

I sat up in my bed and replayed Slim's words again and again in my head. I was blindsided by the whole situation. Slim was a good girl, churchgoing with a strong moral foundation. I admired her faith, professional discipline, and closeness with her family. I wanted to be in a relationship with her because I saw her as somebody I could learn to love. I just never saw infidelity being in the lesson plan. I felt offended, embarrassed, and a bit confused. I was a good man, an attentive father with solid principles. But knowing that she and Ralph dated before we began our relationship I was left to wonder if I was just an easy rebound for her.

JOURNAL ENTRY

More than anything I just want to get it right with somebody who is just as tired of getting it wrong as I am.

There are many different types of "single" when you look at it as a relationship status. Some singles just want to mingle and keep things casual. Some singles are still in love with someone but date others to pass time. And the most common definition of single is: an unmarried man or woman.

After Slim, I decided being single was best for me and I didn't plan on changing my status anytime soon. I can't deny the hope

I had for our relationship; by all definitions of the word, she is a "keeper." But after her actions, I no longer believed that our relationship was something to keep holding onto. It wasn't my first time being cheated on but I knew I wanted it to be my last. I wanted committed companionship. But I took the end of this relationship as a sign that it just wasn't my season for romance.

Oftentimes when I am disappointed, frustrated, or confused about something, writing my thoughts out helps me begin to feel better. I never wrote about relationships to give advice and I did not consider myself to be an expert on the topic. As I filled the pages of my journal, I realized that I had so much I wanted to say. And the more I wrote the less I thought about being cheated on. I didn't feel cheated at all. Instead, I viewed our relationship as a seed of inspiration. One that would pay off sooner than I knew.

Though I didn't consider myself an expert on anything, there are many professional relationship experts who offer a variety of books and services. Most of the content falls under the category of "self-help," which is basically a short way of saying, "Motivation to help people achieve things for themselves." These messages and books serve as inspiration because they encourage the use of one's own effort and resources, rather than being helpless and only relying on others for help. The more I read I started to pick up on commonalities among the writers. Most books offering relationship and love advice usually had author biographies that read "with over twenty years of marriage." I guessed a few were single, but I could not find many. My assumption was: in the world of self-help, single people don't write advice about relationships.

Still the more I wrote in my journal the more I believed the words were meant to be shared, and that this was a concept for a new book. There was a common thread within my words: have a strong relationship with self before anything. Or simply, "Know yourself." The phrase means understanding your personal strengths and weaknesses. Knowing what things and behaviors in life make you joyful, angry, and at ease. These details dictate the quality of every other relationship we have, be it romantic, family, or professional. Though I wanted to be in a relationship, being single gifted me the time to gain a responsible understanding of who I really was and who I wanted to be moving forward in life. With each journal entry I was able to write my thoughts and see my feelings plainly. However, I still wouldn't call it advice. In fact, I didn't know what to call it at all.

Until I named it.

For Single People Who Still Understand the Value of Relationships, released June 1, 2012.

"It looks like you're going to sell well over five hundred copies your first week, son." My mom gave me the news with a bit of astonishment in her voice.

I knew my social media following was growing, and it was affirming to see those people become avid supporters of my new release. It took eight months to sell five hundred copies of *About Something Real*, so this was progress. I watched *For Single People* rise to number one in Amazon's relationship category and seeing the website's "Best Seller" tag beside my name was a dream come true. The book was selling in places I'd never been.

South Africa, Australia, Kenya, France, the Philippines, Japan, and Canada. People were buying copies and sending pictures of their purchase to me on social media. I wanted to call my career counselor from the navy to gloat but instead I hugged my mother. She was the one who believed, was my editor and publishing partner. Together we deserved a moment to celebrate.

College Life Again

In June of 2012 I used my post-9/11 GI Bill to enroll in classes at Tidewater Community College. This bill, put in place after the September 11 terrorist attacks, offers financial assistance for education and training to honorably discharged veterans. It's an extra thank-you to service members who are looking to pursue a degree after active duty. Unlike my freshman year at NSU, I took my time at TCC as a gift. And no uniform was needed for class, no airplane noises or people shouting out orders, and I could leave whenever I wanted to. It beat being on base all day. And after becoming a father, sailor, and smarter person, I actually wanted the instruction. I cultivated some strong study habits over the years just from reading and journaling. Now, the biggest things I wanted to learn were the tools to solidify me as an author and guide me into entrepreneurship full-time.

My favorite class was a public speaking course. My speech at Clemson went well but I knew I needed some training so I was excited to receive whatever tools the professor was willing to offer. Jason Van Gardner, a 6'2" black man in his midthirties, brought unbridled enthusiasm and energy to the class every single day. Charismatic and encouraging, Jason had an approach to teaching that was fresh and dynamic. He was unlike most of the professors I'd encountered. He was like Daniel from NSU. Jason renamed the four walls of our classroom a "learning community." His focus was on creating an environment that made us comfortable enough to share our stories and speak confidently. Whether it was tips to reduce the anxiety in the room or help organizing the structure of our presentations, Jason controlled the flow.

I wanted to have that kind of presence when I spoke in front of a crowd. I used each class as a live practice. I approached every speaking assignment as if I was delivering it to President Obama and other world leaders. I rehearsed my lines, rewrote my key points, and searched for analogies that could serve as comic relief when I stumbled. Public speaking class was both serious and fun for me. The opportunity to be heard, coached, and acknowledged was exactly what I needed in my life.

"Discontent is the catalyst of change," Jason said during the last week of the semester. "When we are restless, frustrated, or uncomfortable enough to the point of discontent, it is at that point that we have the choice or opportunity to do something different, something new, something that will improve our situation. And if we aren't willing to change or look at things from a fresh perspective, then we are left to deal with the same old stuff." I received the message and straight As in the class. Jason helped me to become a better speaker and as a result I was encouraged to continue finding ways to positively impact others.

While *For Single People* sold faster than *About Something Real* and received some acclaim, releasing the book did not solve my financial problems. Self-publishing has its limitations when it comes to distribution, marketing, and overall funding. I thought that signing a book deal with a major

> It reminded me that being uncomfortable or discontented is just a signal that a habit, thought, or behavior needs to change.

publisher would help boost book sales, logistics support, and my overall success as an author. That was the victory I had my sights on. Only, publishers and agents weren't exactly knocking down my door. In fact, it was the complete opposite. Out of the three hundred agents and publishers I queried, many of them said the same thing.

"I'll pass."

But . . . there was another response that always stood out a little more.

"Good luck but not for me." I got this one three times, and I saved each one.

My heart was in these pages, what do you mean it's not for you?

Feelings of self-doubt and rejection began to creep in. Was my work really not good enough? Or was I just asking the wrong people to recognize its value?

The feeling of rejection was hard to ignore. I didn't have

any expectations of becoming Stephen King overnight, but I thought my progress as a self-published author would be more attractive to literary representatives. I did not think getting people to help me would be arduous. I believed in my writing, family and friends supported my books. I thought that meant it was only a matter of time before the rest of the world wanted more. But that's a thought I kept to myself, along with my inbox full of email rejections.

"What are you most proud of? Like . . . when you look back on your life?" It was just us two in the room. The questions had been on my mind for a few days, but I did not know how to ask. With a surge of courage, I leaned up in my chair, facing Papa as he sat on the edge of his hospital bed. He was looking me in my eyes but paused before speaking. Then he looked away slowly, still silent.

The doctors informed us that he would be released to go home under hospice care in the morning. GeGe and my mother were in the hallway discussing the terms and making arrangements. I wanted his answer before they returned but his silence left me in suspense. Then he looked up at me.

"My consistency. I've made my mistakes and learned my lessons. But I'm most proud that I've been consistent. I always got better as a person. That's really all life is about, Robert Brandyn."

"Good news, Daddy, you're coming home. They are going to observe you tonight and Momma and I will be back here first thing in the morning to pick you up." Before I could respond my mom was back in the room. I shook Papa's hand as we left the hospital.

"I love you, man," I said as I released my grip.

My grandfather Robert W. Jewell passed away August 5, 2012, just three days after our conversation. I visited him the day before at my grandparents' house in Camelot. He didn't resemble the strong, independent person he truly was anymore. He barely ate, and lost weight in every area of his body. He was unable to walk or use the bathroom by himself. It was the ugliest moment I'd seen him endure, yet he was surrounded by people who loved him. I watched the women of our family work with the efficiency of a seven-star hotel. Papa's wife, daughters, and granddaughters were all there to help out and make sure he was as comfortable as possible. I held Papa's hand as he slept . . . the same way I held Teo's forearm that day of his accident. They had a similar warmth, almost like a load of towels fresh from the dryer. As I held my grandfather's hand, looking at his face, I thought about leaving my son, Robert, in the world after my death. And I found myself so uncomfortable with our mortality as people.

How quickly life goes from one thing to another . . .
From joy to sadness.
From having to longing.
From life to death.

Watching Papa pass away changed me. It wasn't sudden but it was still unexpected, like with Teo. It seemed unnatural, mysterious, and incredibly uncomfortable, though Papa had been battling cancer for years. I guess we all just truly expected him to win. He embodied the spirit and resilience of a champion fighter. But no champ can stay in the ring forever. Much like no human gets life on Earth forever. We all have our unique moment to be born and our time to die. My grandfather's passing made me think about my own life and the type of person I wanted to be remembered as when I was no longer living. When Teo passed away, I wondered about the spiritual nature of his death. Like how God could let someone so young die so soon. Losing Papa, I found myself thinking about who he was as a person. Like how he made people feel, think, and grow in his seventy years.

I was a month away from turning twenty-five years old. I'm sure if somebody approached Papa when he was twenty-five and told him one day he would have cancer, have his leg amputated after fighting the disease for ten years, and die weighing one hundred and thirty pounds he wouldn't believe them. Just like if someone came to me when I was fifteen and told me that I'd be mourning the death of my best friend at eighteen, a dad by twenty, and at my grandfather's funeral by twenty-five, I wouldn't believe them. I learned anything could happen at any time. Life was going to offer me no guarantees and if I could have just one more conversation with Papa, I believed he would agree on that.

Losing Teo, Papa, my grandmother Ida, and the sailors on

deployment has taught me that dying is natural and normal. Wellness is not limited to quantity of life. Wellness, truly being healthy and fulfilled, is about what a person does with their time throughout the years. It's revealed in the decisions they make and the ones they don't. Death makes you think really hard about the way you're spending your time. And when you lose someone you love and respect, it makes you examine the parts of life that truly matter. It made me reconsider the company I kept, the hobbies I invested in, and the way I treated the people I claimed to value. I knew I could not control when my time to die came, but I wanted to make sure my time alive was spent doing well.

One question continued to repeat itself in my mind: What are people going to remember about me?

Redirection: Channeling the Pain for Good

The two-story redbrick house where my grandparents lived is the first place I ever considered home. Their house has always been the epicenter of my family. Holidays, birthdays, just-because days, it didn't matter. If there was a time to get together and enjoy family, we were doing it at GeGe and Papa's house. The neighborhood is called Camelot with streets named after characters and places from the medieval tale. For me it was just as magical. Most of my family grew up in the neighborhood, both sets of grandparents lived within a five- to ten-minute walk of each other. My mom and her two sisters and my dad Dana and his nine siblings. My aunts and uncles who lived nearby had kids so I was always comfortable outside and had someone to play with. I felt safe and welcome.

Except Camelot wasn't exactly the place to always feel safe and welcome. The neighborhood had a reputation for being tough and the climate of safety would change often and without warning. One day everyone is playing sports together and the next day you couldn't go anywhere without cops swarming or a fight. For the young men in the neighborhood there were three ways to earn your stripes—get money either through robbing or selling drugs, be a standout athlete, or be a ladies' man. Sports and girls were my choice. I kept to myself for the most part and never really had any major problems.

My time in the navy kept me away from Camelot after college. I'd visit here and there but never had enough downtime to catch up with old friends or check in with people I'd known over the years. On one particular trip home I decided to visit the recreation center where I played basketball as a child—the same one I visited after serving my shortened jail sentence. I was hoping to play a few games of basketball while catching up with the many faces that had decorated my life throughout the years. But the reunion was anything but grand. Though the faces were the same, the circumstances were much different.

My visit was underscored with horror story after horror story, usually ending with someone being in jail or on their way home from jail. And these were sons, brothers, my old classmates. Men who were now fathers with kids not much older than my son, missing from a community that needed them all because of poor decisions. "You know how it is out here" was said over and over, as if they had come to accept how things were going. And maybe they had, but I couldn't. I thought about all of my plans for a bright future and how much I needed to stay disciplined. I thought about my eight nights in jail and all of the promises I made to become a better person. I left that chilly September night feeling desperate for change, not just for myself but for my home.

A Letter to the Hearts of My Generation

Love,

I want more for us as a people than the pain we've grown so accustomed to feeling and carrying around. Life isn't meant for suffering. Life isn't about disappointments and fears and isolating ourselves behind walls and false images. There's so much more growing to do. We are all one choice away from a completely different life. Don't live yours discouraged. That is choosing defeat. Things haven't worked out perfectly for you because perfection isn't possible, even excellence isn't appreciated without mistakes.

Your story, your testimony, your life; it all has more value than you know. We were not put here to be islands, we are stronger connected. Greatness isn't something God only gives to a select few, the potential for greatness is in all of us but unfortunately, it's only cultivated by a few. I believe you are still alive and well enough to read these words for a reason. Whatever happened to you didn't kill you. It may have hurt, but it wasn't strong enough to break you so don't allow it to stop you from moving forward.

You are more than your pain. You are more than your heartbreaks. You are more than your mistakes. Your mission on this Earth is not just to survive; your mission is to thrive. Don't let the world intimidate you and get you to believe that you are behind. You are not behind, in fact, you are exactly where you should be. Today, this very moment is the perfect opportunity to make dreams come true. Just commit to work that fulfills you.

Get motivated to do something. If you don't know what your passion or purpose is, start volunteering your time to finding it. Read different books, travel to new places, start actively seeking things that will bring you long-term fulfillment, not just temporary happiness. Success is making sure your lows consistently get higher. Consistent progress is the goal, value your own effort. If you're just chasing money you'll be running in circles the rest of your life. Instead, find something that you're willing to die for, and then live for it. We need more builders!

When you leave this Earth, will your life be remembered? Will you being alive have meant something valuable to your family, your community, or this world? Will people know what was important to you? Will people be better because they knew you?

Service is success.

You have to believe that there is more to life and you have to be courageous enough to pursue whatever that is for you. You deserve joy, you deserve love, and you deserve peace so you have to do whatever is necessary to protect what's important to you. Start giving your time to the things that really matter. Put forth the effort to making your dreams a reality. All we get is time and choices — that's it. Start appreciating the moments that give your life true value.

This world will never be perfect, but it should be better because you exist. I believe in the greatness of your heart and it's time to start healing each other. Let's show the world a new way.

Rob Hill Sr.

Thousand Kings Walk

There's no one set formula for success. However, there are some attributes of leadership that are universal and often about finding ways of encouraging people to combine their efforts, talents, insights, enthusiasm, inspiration, and resources to work together toward a common goal.

The week of my twenty-fifth birthday I founded the Thousand Kings Foundation, Inc. That quote became the mission statement of the Thousand Kings Walk. My initial goal was to get 1,000 men and boys to come out and to raise $1,000 for scholarships. The march would be a spark of hope for Camelot, a chance to see the community working together. I wanted our mothers, wives, daughters, aunts, and whatever other support systems they had to come out as well. I was encouraged by my parents to think even bigger. Suddenly my focus shifted from being more than just an author, to now an organizer, ready to serve the community that had long molded me.

With seven months left to plan, I secured Mount Trashmore Park in Virginia Beach as the official event location for the march. June 1, 2013, would be the date. I drafted an event proposal to offer potential supporters a basic sense of the march and information on how they could help. I started with my "Thoughts for the Day" email group then took to social media to help spread the word. Facebook, Twitter, Tumblr, Instagram, LinkedIn, YouTube, and every site in between. (Between social media and the TFTD email group my following had grown to around ten thousand people.) If there was a wall or message board, I posted details there and asked others to do the same. The goal was to make the event a topic of conversation for those who wanted to see positive change and more constructive fellowship within their communities.

The feedback was tremendous, with many people who instantly committed to participating. I increased my goal to 5,000 people in attendance and $10,000 in scholarship money to donate to young men ages twelve to seventeen. I felt joy in the work that was being done. Securing event insurance, press coverage, vendor permits, security, and more was not easy, but the mission made the process undeniably meaningful. I was beginning to feel like I was living my purpose.

With unwavering enthusiasm I dedicated the rest of 2012

and the first five months of the new year to organizing the Thousand Kings Walk. The energy was contagious, and I knew it was important to make sure I talked face-to-face with as many people as I could. By the end of March, I'd put almost seventeen thousand miles on my 2006 Honda Accord driving to speaking engagements in Virginia, North Carolina, Georgia, Maryland, D.C., New York City, and more. I visited churches, group homes, detention centers, universities, clubs, elementary, middle, and high schools; it didn't matter where I had to go, as long as I could find a few people who would take some time to listen to what I had to say. I told my story, my mistakes, and how I'd grown over the years. I told them about the importance of the Thousand Kings Walk and my mission to revitalize our communities through love, knowledge, and service. At each stop more and more people supported the campaign and promised to join us in person on June 1.

I hired Marque Robinson, a young photographer I knew from Portsmouth, Virginia, to accompany me as I traveled. I had worked with him once before at my first book signing, and we began to grow as friends. By hired, I mean I explained my vision for the walk, told him that I couldn't pay his fee, and he still agreed to do the work because he believed in what I was doing. We took on a big brother–little brother relationship and spent every day together. If Marque could help with something, he was right there and it began to feel like I had a true partner in the journey.

As the momentum built, so did the expenses: travel, gas,

lodging, food, unexpected car repairs, and tolls. Occasionally I'd get a small speaking honorarium but most of my speaking events I did for free. Funds were scarce and my to-do list was growing minute by minute. The pressure was mounting. But I was resourceful. To help raise money I started selling T-shirts through an online store that I set up on BigCartel.com. I got a few different designs made with the Thousand Kings logo and set them on the front of the shirts. I let people know that all of the money from shirt sales would be used in support of the Thousand Kings Walk. The shirts sold out, covering all the event costs . . . and all I needed was a plan to raise $10,000 for scholarships.

When you discover your mission, you will feel it calling you. It will fill you with enthusiasm and a burning desire to get to work on it. Until then be a sponge, soak up new information and always ask questions. The more self-aware you become, the more balanced your life will be.

I ended my speech at the youth juvenile detention center in Norfolk with those words. The room was filled with about fifty young men and their counselors. Though I wasn't in Chesapeake, all of them could've come from Camelot. Staring out at their faces—defeated, lost, hurt. The moment reminded me of that night at the rec center. I could see their eyes soften as I spoke. I could sense hope in their questions. I couldn't save them or erase their circumstances, but I could be someone new to say, "I believe in you." Most of them would still be incarcerated on the day of the march, but I left hoping they heard something that gave them hope for creating a better future when their day came.

In April I kicked off the official Thousand Kings Walk scholarship contest. I split the writing requirements into four areas of focus: purpose, identity, legacy, and love. Each essay entry had to answer four questions: What is your purpose in life? What is your identity, or what does your name mean? What kind of legacy will you leave? What is love to you? The essay could either be submitted through email or by snail mail. We received over 200 submissions. I didn't want perfect essays, rather I just wanted genuine responses. I wanted their words to feel authentic.

Dear Mr. Rob,

Thank you for coming to speak to us. You really said a lot of things I can relate to. I made a lot of decisions that landed me in here but I feel like life hasn't really given much choice. At one point my whole family was together, as time passed, my dad was spending more and more time away from the house. Leaving my mother who can't read to take care of us. Then my older brother was being seen less and less. I had to become the man of the house. Help pay rent, help my little sister with her homework. I had to buy my own school clothes because my mom never had a job. I never gave up but I did have to take risks. Two of my biggest risks landed me in the detention center, both were life threatening. The first time the power of prayer got me home. I got back in school and played varsity football. Family still having problems with rent and food caused me

*to come back to the detention center where I am now with
5 felonies. I want to be the first person in my family to go
to college. I will not give up and I will go back to school
and finish my 11th grade year. Then graduate in 2014
with my class. I just need a good half time talk and your
speech helped me. I am motivated to go to college and
make something of myself.*

A sixteen-year-old wrote these words. Reading this letter among the other submissions nearly moved me to tears. Somebody should've been there to guide and protect him.

On May 29, 2013, just two days out, the total scholarship contribution was at $8,000. Over 400 people donated through a crowdfunding tool attached to my social media. We were still $2,000 short. Then I got the call from Pun, a very popular DJ in the area and a supporter of the walk. I held weekly meet-ups to generate support and paid him to provide the music. On this call, Pun inquired about how much we were short from the goal and I told him $2,000. He asked me to meet him by Norfolk State University, and as I walked up to his truck, he counted out the $2,000 he'd raised through his own efforts.

We'd made it.

I looked around at the NSU campus, remembering who I was the last time I was there. Fresh out of high school, so lost, so hurt. And there I was seven years later. I'd taken a chance on myself, when before I was so unwilling. I was now in position to make a difference in my community. This was victory.

JOURNAL ENTRY

Don't let temporary struggle turn you into a quitter. Be diligent and don't stop until you accomplish what you set out
to do. Don't allow your emotions to drain your enthusiasm.

When June 1, 2013, arrived it felt like Christmas morning. I got to Mount Trashmore around eight a.m. I looked out over the empty space. *What if no one shows?* I couldn't shake that bit of fear inside of me. Sure, I'd worked tirelessly to get commitments from well over 5,000 people. *But . . . what if no one shows? What if this doesn't happen? What if?* Though I had my concerns I still needed to set up for the event. A little more than a hundred volunteers arrived to help. My mom and my sister Elise coordi-nated and directed everyone as needed. At 11:45 a.m. we began with my greeting.

> *Welcome to the first ever Thousand Kings Walk. Our goal here is to inspire, impact, and influence people to live extraordinary lives. Let's choose to embrace one another through hugs, laughter, and smiles. This is a dream come true for me but this event is for us, the entire community.*

I introduced each of the scholarship winners just before we got started and the crowd cheered for them in a way I'll never forget. The young men lit up with smiles of gratitude. Their community saw them, which is no small thing. Each one of us, no matter our race, gender, or economic background, we all just want to be seen. And I could tell that the recognition meant more to them than the money.

The walk itself was along a mile-and-a-half paved trail. I lined up at the beginning with the scholarship winners beside me. Over my shoulder were thousands of people, ready to walk behind us, follow our lead, push us forward should we grow tired, encourage us should we lose hope, and find us should we get lost. It was magical. As we neared the halfway mark I asked the boys to turn around and look at what they were leading. I asked them how it felt to know this many people showed up for them and one responded with, "It feels like I have to be great in life, like I can't let all these people down."

"I wish my dad was here," another responded.

"Everybody you need is right here," I assured him. "Spend today being proud of yourself."

When the boy mentioned his dad, his words pinched a nerve because everyone I wanted to be at the walk was there except for one person, my son. His pre-K graduation was the same day and after many talks with the school there was no changing it. But I needed him to be there with me. I wanted him to feel the experience. This was a once-in-a-lifetime thing. Sequoyah promised to drop him off as soon as it ended. I paid close attention to the time as we continued to walk.

My mother greeted me as we approached the finish line, her eyes filled with tears. "How does it feel?" she whispered in my ear. "Five thousand people showed up for something you organized." It was the first confirmation that we'd hit our goal. Along with my sister Elise and other volunteers, my mom had been at the entrance keeping count of every visitor. All I could do was say thank you, to her, to God, to the community for their trust. I couldn't thank everyone enough, my family, the volunteers, the park staff, the organizations, leaders, and participants who drove from New York, Philadelphia, D.C., North Carolina, Georgia, and many other places.

As we brought the event to a close, I delivered a speech:

Thank you all for being here. Today is monumental and it's a blessing to have each one of you here to share it.

We must strive for excellence and we cannot get tired in our pursuit of greatness. This journey isn't for those who don't expect to win.

The fight may be challenging but one thing we will not do is quit.

Where we are outmanned, we will outwit. Where we are cornered, we will fight. Where we are passed off, we will push through.

One thing we will not do is quit.

Our will creates the way. Our purpose guides us on the path. Our sacrifice secures success.

There is no doubt that we will win, for victory has been promised, the only question is how.

Will we win alone, and have no one to share it with?
Will we win for self, and watch others fail, die, and hurt
for generations?

How will we win? And at what cost?

I ask you, who are we?

Who are we not to make history?

Who are we not to be moguls, geniuses, and visionaries?

Who are we not to want it all and to be audacious
enough to believe we deserve it?

Who are we not to be timeless and celebrated?

Who are we not to redefine the standard?

Who says we have to be "normal"?

None of us were born to be normal; mediocrity is a
choice just as greatness is.

We can't force anybody to be great or to live up to their
potential.

But who are we not to chase our dreams?

Who are we not to start our own businesses?

Who are we not to test the limits and boundaries and
surpass all expectations?

Who says we have to be "normal"?

None of us were born to chill; we are all here for change.

In each of us there is a unique gift,

Something special for us to leave our unique mark on
the world.

Who says we have to dumb it down so people don't feel
uncomfortable?

Who says that we aren't supposed to be the movers and
the shakers?

Who says that we can't lead and influence thousands to live extraordinary lives?

Who says we have to be "normal"?

We were all put here for a divine reason,

And there is unlimited power and potential in each one of us.

We aren't here to be swayed by fears and doubts.

We are here to conquer, we are here to flourish, we are here to prosper.

Who says we have to be "normal"?

We are here as signs of God's grace, his mercy, and his remarkable favor.

We are beautiful, talented, and blessed beyond measure.

And who are we not to be?

We aren't normal,

We are here to be legendary.

We are here to inspire.

We are here to give, to sacrifice, to lay it all on the line for those that are to come after us. This world should be better because we are here, it should be changed because of our presence and if we aren't crazy enough to believe that then we are leaving the generations to come with a life full of suffering.

And that is unacceptable.

To my men, my Kings. It is time for us to rise. It is time for us to grow. It is time for us to give more of ourselves. Our Queens need us, our communities need us, our future needs us.

The great Martin Luther King Jr. said, "A man who won't die for something is not fit to live." So I ask you, what is it you're living for? Is it bigger than you or are you only living for what can benefit you? If I was to die today it would mean that my son would have a better life. If I was to die it would mean more opportunities for those around me. If I was to die, it would be so you could live better.

A male that is not willing to sacrifice for the greater success of his people is not a man at all.

Whether we see it or not, and let's not be misled, us being here is not the victory, this is the beginning. What we've started here, the history we've made, the lives we've touched, the thousands that have been inspired, this walk is just the signifying of our promise to commit toward building a more prosperous future.

This walk is a recommitment to family. This is the return of our village!!!

Last summer while battling for his life, I asked my grandfather, the late Robert Wayne Jewell, what he was most proud of and, after thinking for a minute, his answer was simple, "I'm most proud of my consistency." And in that moment, I received a revelation.

We as a people must be so consistent in our love; in our pursuit of happiness; in our commitment to excellence that we cannot be doubted. We must be driven, passionate, and faithful on our journey. And when we're asked why we deserve it, we'll simply say, "Our consistency has earned it for us."

To every mother wondering if she'll have help, look around . . . there's hope.

To every son wishing he had somebody who cares, look around . . . there's hope.

To every person who's lacking in faith, look around . . . We are blessed!

Robert Jr. arrived less than ten minutes after my speech and all felt right with the world. Side by side we thanked everyone for coming out. I soaked up every single moment, savoring each face, each hug, each step; it was better than I ever could've imagined. I felt free, accomplished, and like the leader I always knew I could be. In that moment, I know that faith was stronger than fear. I knew I had the discipline needed to be excellent at the work that's important to me. I chose to trust what was purposed for me. I didn't quit. I believed. I stayed committed and because of that I found success.

And I was hungry for more.

CHAPTER NINE

Adjusting My Scope

Seventeen dollars. That's what I had in my bank account the day after the Thousand Kings Walk. While I was riding the high of bringing my community together, helping to restore a feeling of hope, I couldn't even afford a full tank of gas for myself.

The good news: I moved back in with my parents and did not have to pay monthly rent. When I did make money, I had to be smart and use it wisely.

The bad news: It takes money to make money. And the income from my books was not producing a level of funds that can be easily multiplied . . . yet!

"Nothing wrong with my aim, just gotta change the target."
—Jay-Z

Though I wasn't seeing my dollars add up as quickly as I wanted them to, I was learning better ways to structure and organize myself as an entrepreneur. There's this thing in management referred to as the "project scope." It is the work that must be done to deliver a desired result. To get to the next level in business it would be necessary to generate more streams of income and to keep growing as a writer. The latter I could handle. I knew the only way to blossom as a writer was to write more. But generating the type of income that matched my salary in the navy? That was going to require me focusing my aim on the right targets.

The first bull's-eye was on my heart.

Unchecked personal issues can have a cascading effect on our ability to accept and give intimacy. I often ignored my feelings about painful life memories and used my energy to push uncomfortable thoughts to the back of my mind. If that did not work, and I became overwhelmed by a problem or my emotions, I would shut down and deal with things the way I did on deployment. Only, you can't build an intimate relationship the same way you approach a deployment. A relationship thrives off of openness, transparency, and communication. Sure, we communicated on deployment but it wasn't the "your feelings matter" kind. While away, it was practical to suppress my feelings, thoughts, and complaints to focus on the mission and work productively. At home, doing those things only hurt my chances of building a serious relationship.

"Do you trust yourself?"

I asked the question on the first line of a journal entry. I knew I had confidence in me, some hope, even some determination to succeed. But as I stared at the question, I could not honestly say any of that amounted to trust. I continued . . .

"I want to be on point with me, secure about who I am, and unafraid to be open . . ."

I've realized when we pray for patience, we aren't given the gift immediately, instead we are given more opportunities to be patient. When we ask for strength, we aren't given mighty muscles and superpowers, instead we are given opportunities to be courageous, creative, and disciplined. In a way my journal entry that day was a prayer for security and banishment of my fear. I now realize that I was asking for an opportunity to face the giants suppressing my heart. And I'm grateful because I needed a chance to search within and scope the true contents of my target.

The second bull's-eye was on my mind.

So about those giants suppressing my heart? Being broke. Fear of losing my son. Well, another one of them was post-traumatic stress disorder or PTSD. It can occur following the experience or witnessing of a life-threatening event. Possible events include: military combat, natural disasters, terrorist incidents, serious accidents, physical/sexual assault in adult- or childhood. As far as experiences go, I checked off *all of the above* and it was hard for me to think of anyone I knew that hadn't experienced at least two major traumatic events in their lifetime. Still, very few people around me were talking about dealing with the trauma, and I wasn't eager to start the conversation. In the words of Solange Knowles, "I tried to keep myself busy. I ran around in circles, think I made myself dizzy. I slept it away. I sexed it away. I read it away."

Any conversation around my mental health made me feel uncomfortable. I'd rather someone believe I was moody and emotional than to think I had PTSD or that I wasn't in control of myself. I didn't want a condition and I wasn't looking to visit a doctor for a diagnosis either. When you're a veteran, as soon as you mention those four letters, people start fidgeting and looking at you as if you're going to randomly hurt them. I never had any desire to hurt anyone, but I do believe not being honest about the way I felt was doing more harm than good to me.

"Stop all that crying and man up. Men don't cry." I don't remember the first person who said it to me, but I do remember hearing this anytime I or other young boys cried. Whatever it was that made us want to cry, we weren't supposed to feel that because, well, we were boys. And I kept those same principles going as I grew into manhood. Often mirroring the stone-cold demeanor of the older black men I observed. *No smiles, eyes serious, and walk like you don't give a fuck. You can feel whatever you want, just don't show weakness.*

But the more I wrote, the more giants I faced and the more everything I felt inside started to show. Suppressing emotions did not work for me. Holding in, holding back, or holding out, none of it worked. Expressing myself was the only comforting solution, and to do so I had to let go of my fear and release my attachment to the events of my past. I did it piece by piece and I always felt better after acknowledging my true thoughts. Writing was my first therapy.

Aside from writing, I have a passion for finding great songs. Music can create a powerful impact on us throughout the day. Upbeat songs can boost energy and slower, more rhythmic songs can calm and soothe the mind. Writing became a therapeutic tool for me, but I do not need therapy every moment of the day. I love to listen to music because poets like Jay-Z remind me that "life is for living, not living uptight." But I never thought that I'd be making music for myself. I knew the process wasn't easy. Nevertheless, I was ready to try my hand at it. The idea came after talking with some friends about reading and how they struggled to sit still through an entire book. "I'm always on the go. Sometimes I just want to put my headphones on and listen to something inspirational. I don't always have time to read a book," one friend remarked.

"Well, what if I take my poems or messages and put them over a beat. Would you listen to that?" I asked, wondering if I had just stumbled across a new medium to grow my brand and attract nontraditional readers to my work.

"Do it and let me hear it. I'll tell you if it's dope."

"Bet!" I replied.

I immediately started reaching out to a few people I knew in the Virginia area who produced music and who had a place to record. I was referred to Dante Lewis, who had a studio he worked out of in Virginia Beach. The first session was free, and I used money from my book sales to schedule a few additional sessions with him at a discounted rate. He could tell I was new to the entire studio experience. I decided to start with poems I'd already written and revised them to repeat a catchy phrase or two. I was surprised to be so nervous in the recording booth, but it helped ease my anxiety using pieces that I was familiar with. Some of them were poems I'd written during my early NSU days, others were pieces I started on deployment, and some came from my blog. Reciting the words took me back to the moments and relationships that inspired them. After I read the poetry, I'd leave the booth and let Dante build the music behind it.

"So what are we calling this?" Dante asked as I was leaving the studio one afternoon.

"It'll come to me," I replied.

One day the title did come to me. I called it, *The Audacity of a Good Heart*. So many people around me had given up on finding a good partner. Many had decided that love, healthy relationships, and commitment were no longer for them. I knew I didn't want to reach that point myself. I wanted to believe differently about what was ahead for my heart, for my love life. Yes, I had some relationships that did not work out. But they only inspired me to strengthen my weaknesses. Sure, I made some mistakes and faced painful consequences. Still, even those missteps, I recognize as the moments where I was able to gain some balance in my life and heighten my self-awareness. Regardless of where I went wrong in relationships, my ultimate intention was to be someone who knew how to love like rain, ready to calm any fire. Unfortunately, when I poured my love the fire always moved, and I usually just felt empty afterward. It was like what I was giving could never fill the cup.

I Had a Dream

I had a dream I could change you
Not just because I could make you into who I wanted you
to be
But because I finally got to see you as the "you" I always
knew you could be

In my dream, all the potential turned into promise
I didn't have to motivate you because you were already
motivated
I didn't have to teach you because you were so eager to
learn, that you were always ahead . . .

See, I had a dream I could change you
And that's exactly what I did
I changed you
For US

I had a dream I could change you
I took your weaknesses and I strengthened them
I changed the parts of your body that you didn't like,
and made you love them
That way I wouldn't have to hear you complain about
flaws I saw nothing but beauty in

In my dream, the insecurities turned into confidence
I told you that you were beautiful and you actually
believed me
I told you that I loved you and you didn't question it

See, I had a dream that I could change you
And that's exactly what I did
I changed you
For US

I had a dream I could change you
I took away all your fears and I replaced them with
courage
I took away all the trust issues and I replaced them with
faith

In my dream, the doubts turned into desires
You stopped caring about getting hurt and you started
wondering how to accept love
You stopped questioning and you started believing
I gave you an outlook on life that allowed you to let me in

See, I had a dream I could change you
And that's exactly what I did
I changed you
For US

I had a dream I could change you
But . . . I woke up without you

I changed you into a person that you couldn't recognize
Somebody that you were scared to see
A version of you that you just weren't ready to be

In my dream, it all seemed so simple
I could change you, and we could be WE
But in changing you, it allowed me to see
It's pointless settling for a person I'll only ever meet
in my dreams

So instead of changing you,
I had to change how I felt about you,
And move on . . .
For ME!

—TRACK 6 ON *AUDACITY OF A GOOD HEART*

The Audacity of a Good Heart was completed as my first studio album and the recording process became another form of therapy for me. One that I wasn't even aware that I needed. My mind was in a better place.

"Do you trust yourself?" The question remained alone in my journal, only now, I had my answer . . .

"Yes, I trust myself!"

The third bull's-eye was on my passion.

Once again, my journal entries and personal reflections of

self-discovery became the topic for a book. With my second release, *For Single People*, I opened the door for a discussion about the benefits of singleness, healthy dating habits, and the pillars of strong relationships. With my third book, I had an opportunity to take the conversation even further. It was time to use my new sense of trust to encourage others enduring their own battles with opening up to love, being loved, and healing from hurtful experiences. I named it, *I Got You: Restoring Confidence in Love and Relationships*

This book isn't about playing a game to get what you want. It's about you looking at yourself and finding ways to learn how to grow as an individual. I cannot tell you every single step you should take to get you to where you are trying to go in life. But what I can do is make sure you have enough confidence to trust your own judgments, regardless of past mistakes. I want you to understand that it's okay to be exactly where you are right now, whether you are single or in a relationship. Appreciate where your journey is taking you, but be able to identify areas that need to change. I want you to read this book and have a better understanding of the present. I want you to know that trying to get it right is a constant process. We never arrive at a place of knowing it all. For as long as we are alive, we are challenged to grow, learn, evolve, and mature. Love is a decision, not a destination. It's not something you stumble upon. You must choose to walk in it, give in to it, and become it. Each of us travels a different path to find the love we are searching for. Some find what they are looking for instantly, while others must jump over a few hurdles before realizing they have finally found something special. In essence, we are all just working toward what we believe we deserve—our fair chance at love and happiness.

I picked my twenty-sixth birthday as the day of the release for *I Got You* and *The Audacity of a Good Heart* album. I've always seen the day as my personal New Year's. Dropping two passion projects was my version of ringing it in with a bang. I didn't want any gifts that birthday, instead I encouraged friends and family to support my projects. Both releases combined sold over 5,000 copies in the first week. I hadn't sold 5,000 books total with my first two. It was the biggest release of my career up until that point. I couldn't have been prouder.

Financially, I was far from my seventeen-dollar days. My books were the leverage I needed to grow my income, let people know who I was, what I believed, and the causes that were important to me. For the next two years I toured all over the US doing speaking engagements, and my calendar was full.

The fourth bull's-eye was on my spirit.

In August of 2014, JustCurious.com's owner, Lelo Boyana, invited me to headline their annual Love Conference in Johannesburg, South Africa. This would be my second international speaking event. The first was on campus at the University of

Toronto, in Ontario, Canada. I'd done over fifty North American speaking engagements, but this was my first invitation from South Africa. My sister Elise worked tirelessly for months with Lelo to make sure everything was in place for a smooth and productive trip. Elise could not come with me, but one person had to be there, I needed her close, and I called her as soon as things were finalized.

"Hey, Mom, it's your son . . . Guess what?" I said over the phone.

"Boy, I know who you are. What's up, you just won the lotto? I always knew it would happen. How much, 200 million? 300? 4? I mean how high you want me to go?"

She had me laughing out loud like only she can. I continued . . .

"Listen, you beautiful black Queen you, whom I love and adore . . ."

"Uh-oh, how much is your bond? Something is up," she said jokingly before being silent.

Anytime she's playful, I soak it up. And for good reason. She's been the backbone of our family and we rarely afforded her any time to be carefree. The moment to tell her was here.

"Okay, tell me, son, I'm done guessing." she said.

"I'm taking you to South Africa. The whole trip is paid for. All you have to do is pack and get on the plane with me. We out!"

We arrived in Johannesburg five days before the conference and spent the first few days doing press, promoting the conference, and taking in the amazing city and surrounding countryside. I interviewed with every major TV and radio station that would have me. I made my debut on national TV that week, prompting the conference to become the #1 trending topic on Twitter in South Africa during my speech. My mother was right there with me to see and receive it all. I'd steal glances at her as we rode through Johannesburg and Soweto. Her laugh was deeper, like it came from her soul. My mother's life has been dedicated to her family. She always put others before herself, whether it was me or my siblings, or my aunts and cousins, GeGe, or Papa when he was alive. It didn't matter. When I saw her stare out the window at all the black and brown faces, the vibrant colors, the sounds of bustling life, I hoped that she was thinking about herself. Not in a self-consumed way, but more me hoping she still connected with parts of Monique that were completely separate from being a mom, wife, or anything else to anyone. I saw her glow and it made me hope she forever kept pieces of these moments inside.

That Saturday I spoke to a sold-out auditorium of 600 in the Wanderers building at The Forum.

"Hope, forgiveness, and patience are necessary when healing emotional scars. Yes, hurt people hurt people but we have a choice to be more than just hurt people. We can face the hurt, disappointment, and sadness—we can say to it, 'I'm free, you can't control me.'"

I used to tell myself "I can't take another this" or "I can't take another that" a lot. Whether it was losing a loved one, disappointment in romance, or a career setback. I told myself what I couldn't take so much that I started to doubt what was inside of me. I didn't stay sharp and I started to let unhealthy things affect my self-esteem. But every time I look back on the things I thought would break me, I realize that I made it through. And I got better because of it. I'm able to love who I'm becoming because I'm no longer doubting who I am . . . I am no longer a victim in my heart. I'm strong enough, wise enough, and great enough to face anything that's thrown my way.

I've been hurt before, yes, love has taught me many lessons. But I am not broken, I will not be broken, and neither will you. Healed people heal people.

—EXCERPT FROM SPEECH

We left Johannesburg on a high. Throughout my time there I became invigorated by the people, the food, and the evolving culture of the city. The traveler spirit inside me had found another city that could feel like home.

The fifth bull's-eye was on my gift.

I enjoy helping and serving people, so touring and speaking gave me the perfect opportunity to do so. I visited cities like D.C., Atlanta, Miami, New York, Chicago, Seattle, and Los Angeles doing over 150 speaking engagements. It was always enlightening to meet my readers face-to-face. I often found their stories eerily familiar. Their battles with depression, heartache, abandonment, and learning to love all felt like different versions of my journey. I saw myself in their eyes. I heard and recognized the heaviness in their voice. But as we would part ways, I felt their faith, motivation, and resilience for building a better life. I was not attracting just anybody to these events, people were coming because they felt a specific purpose and recognized a piece of themselves in my words. We were mirrors for each other.

These intuitive experiences improved my skills as a writer and molded me into a better person. For the first time, I felt like a whole man. Any moment before, I was a boy, pretending, shifting, but never truly dancing in the full bloom of my essence. Finally, I was most comfortable being present. Not looking back. Not dreaming ahead.

I'm living in the right now. And my scope only adjusts to focus on my target. And my adventure is still only just beginning.

CHAPTER TEN

Love Is Really All That Matters

I did not have a big picture in mind when I left my parents' home at seventeen. I knew pieces of who I was but I had no vision for my future self. I did not envision joining the navy, being an author, Johannesburg, or the thousands of people I've been able to serve throughout my life. Still there was a divine plan that was always working and a true reason I experienced certain things. While I was in motion—learning, loving, healing—it was hard to see how my painful experiences would help me down the line. Now I look back and I see how losing a friend like Teo would make me want to raise $10,000 in scholarships and do the Thousand Kings Walk. I see how having a mother like mine would inspire me to write books, to learn how to publish, and to teach people what I've seen and experienced. I see how the love of two dads like Dana and Frank could mold me into the father that I am to my son. I see how having intellectual, outspoken women as my sisters and cousins to learn from could help me feel confident enough to express and articulate my thoughts and emotions so publicly. I see it all now.

Yes, I enrolled thirteen times in eleven different schools in twelve grades. That's a lot of moving for anyone. But what I gained by observing, adapting, and feeling out of place in those different classrooms was the strength to think for myself and be my own person. As my family moved, I was exposed to people of different cultures, nations, and religions. On every report card I received, "Great student but talkative in class." And the remark was true, I've always had something to say. Rather than shut down and mope over the schools, relationships, or places I lived, I now choose to be curious about the present. I grow because I choose to ask questions, test boundaries, and take risks. From Virginia to London to Toronto, even throughout the United States, I feel at home in my own skin. I'm not lost and nothing I need is missing. Even when I'm uncertain about the path ahead I still know wherever the journey leads me I'm going to find something to learn, someone to love, or somewhere to be.

When I learn, the energy in my spirit encourages me to teach others what I know. When I love and support myself, my soul urges me to be more caring of the people around me. I know wherever I go, whomever I meet, and whatever conversation happens—it all occurs for a reason. That's just the way life works.

I'm still that "single person who understands the value of relationships." Yet I'm evolving, and no longer just a wandering romantic. The piece of my heart that wants marriage, committed partnership, and intimacy with another is alive and optimistic. I look forward to connecting with a woman and knowing our souls were meant to be aligned for a purpose greater than us. A woman the world can truly recognize as my wife. I still write in my journal to her often.

JOURNAL ENTRY

When I Fall

When I fall in Love again I'll know it was by choice
I'll know it was because I searched for it and it found me
And I'll know that I chose to receive it

If by chance my relationship fails
I don't want to be the person that hates Love
I want to take accountability for the things I could've done better

*I want to acknowledge those times where I could have
compromised but didn't
Where I could have given but didn't
And where I should have listened but didn't*

*I don't want to be the person who forever blames Love
for my shortcomings
I don't want her to be the girl who turns bitter because I
couldn't love her better
I don't want us to be the ones who gave up when it was
time to put work in*

*I want to be real and realize that Love isn't responsible
for when I spoke in anger
Or the times I lashed out in revenge and spite
Or even the painful times I've blindfolded myself from
the truth with fear*

*I want to be the person who acknowledges my
imperfections
Who accepts my wrongs and weaknesses
But know that Love is still just as perfect as God
designed it to be*

*I want my partner to understand that we complicated
things
We ran from chances
And that we made mistakes*

I want it to be understood that we tried our best
I want her to know that we loved and learned
And that we don't fall short just because we loved and
lost

I want it to be known that we chose to give pieces of
ourselves that were priceless
We chose compassion, understanding, and trust
Over fear, doubt, and insecurity

I want us to know that we did what real lovers do
I want to trust that even though we didn't give perfectly
that we still gave our all
I want to believe we kissed before good nights and said
I love you before goodbyes

More than anything I want us to have faith
That as long as we're still breathing
We'll live to Love another day.

I haven't reached the point where I have love, relationships, or business all figured out and I'm not sure I ever will. I have, however, reached a point where I embrace the full responsibility that comes with my life.

I will make mistakes as I grow. I've made many along the way. I have hated, judged, lost friends from being too vocal, fought

> **Perfection is not a requirement for my fulfillment.**

family for being too different, and mistreated myself by doing wrong when knowing better. I've caused my share of headaches. Still, I never wanted to be defined as a person by those decisions. I never wanted the sum of my character to be limited to the choices I made due to inexperience, emotion, or impulse. Things change fast in life. We lose best friends in car accidents, the people we see as mentors die, and sometimes we can barely recognize ourselves through the fog of heartbreak. Pain is a powerful teacher, let me tell you, and it molded much of my initial responses when I was bruised emotionally. Before, my instincts were to keep moving, to not look back, to never show how I feel. Now I understand that it is okay to stop moving when you're no longer in alignment with your purpose. Sometimes slowing down is a power move, and the ability to pace ourselves is proof of maturity. It's okay to deal with emotional trauma and even to look back on the past with full acceptance. It's okay to stop living for approval. I don't share all of my career highlights and I don't hide every emotional low. I'm enjoying growth, not pursuing anyone else's vision of a perfect life.

> **Success is the ability to look at my reflection in the mirror and choose love.**

Before I adjusted my scope, I believed success and security to be defined by pieces like money, acclaim, and prominence. After focusing in on myself, I understood success to be much more about peace of mind, collaboration, and self-mastery.

That choice, that subtle but powerful decision to love, has changed everything I believed was possible in life.

> *Rob Hill Sr. never finished college. Until three years ago, he was in the Navy, dreaming of making writing his full-time profession. He sent out daily self-improvement emails called Thoughts for the Day, first to 22 people, eventually to 3,000. His first book, a self-help offering called* About Something Real, *expanded on the emails, but it sold poorly—just 500 copies in eight months. To increase sales, he began driving from campus to campus and church to church, reading and speaking. Without realizing it, he joined the swelling ranks of writers who earn a living primarily through their speaking engagements, which feed into the writing career. Hill's next book made it to the top of Amazon's "relationship" category, and he has now written three others, all self-published, two of which are only available as audiobooks in an innovative style—like spoken-word records with beats behind them. His latest debuted at No. 22 on the Billboard gospel chart. "I'm not depending on anyone to sell the book for me," he says. "And I'm versatile. Nobody gets a higher percentage of sales than I do."*
>
> —THE NEW YORK TIMES MAGAZINE

I've learned when something extraordinary happens to a person in life the best choice is to embrace it and enjoy the ride. Don't second guess your favor. It is an empowering decision to believe that great things should be happening for you, because they should. Many times I've had imposter syndrome, that painful inability to internalize my accomplishments and even a consistent fear of being exposed as a fraud.

What am I doing writing books about relationships?

Why am I on this stage speaking about my experiences? What makes me so different?

If they knew my past would I still be invited to the White House, asked to appear on TV shows, or printed in the *New York Times Magazine*?

The answer: I don't know. But what I do know is that it all happened. I don't need to think about it anymore than that, I only need to be thankful.

I've been asked in interviews, "How do you stay motivated in pursuit of your goals?"

The answer: It's that piece of me that knows, in any moment, life can offer something extraordinary. I just have to be willing to recognize it.

I did not know how to share my story and it took a lot of time to figure out which parts I would offer in these pages. Not out of shame for anything I've lived, but because I'm so proud of who I've become and even more protective of the people I love. The road to self-acceptance is not always lined with the apologies we deserve, or the support that makes it easy to fill deep potholes like feelings of abandonment, inadequacy, and anxiety.

What propels us the farthest in life are those silent powerful shifts we make within. The moments when nobody is clapping, no cameras are flashing, but we are still there, believing, manifesting, and putting in the work. Writing this book was a chance for me to continue my self-work, and in the time it's taken to complete this, I feel like a new person. I'm no longer dancing in the gray. Now I'm changing the picture quality and adding colors, texture, and vibrancy to my life. It's my choice to continuously welcome growth, love, and joy into my mind, heart, and spirit. When I make that shift, I know I am living in my highest gear.

JOURNAL ENTRY

What would you do if you were not afraid to be rejected, or to accept and recognize yourself? You would be free and you would enjoy the love you have for yourself and others.

So what was missing all along? What was that final piece for me in the puzzle to be whole?

Love.

Love is what I feel when I choose self-acceptance, and to be confident and honest about my emotions. Love is what surrounds me and replenishes me when I fall into my pits of fear and rejection. Love is what breaks the bond I have with my mistakes, bad decisions, and unhealthy relationships. Love is strength. It is a bridge. It allowed my spirit to be free again. Love is the first piece and the last piece. The missing piece that makes me whole.

Another big piece that I was missing was trust.

Trust in myself.

Trust in relationships, building a career, and being a good father.

Throughout our lives we are given opportunities to become our best selves. But when there are missing pieces we jump into the world, daring and reaching for a version of ourselves that we cannot access. Then one day it just sinks in. You realize that the pieces were inside of you waiting to be discovered. In my quest to define personal truths, and to learn how to trust myself, I had to master confidence, faith, self-awareness, patience, and forgiveness. My challenges and disappointments forced me to evolve. Once I learned to trust, I began building stronger relationships with the people in my life.

I used to believe I would always regret not having a close relationship to Dana. But somehow, raising a son of my own has brought Dana and me closer and strengthened our relationship. I now know firsthand what it's like to be a young father at twenty, merely discovering yourself as an individual and now responsible for guiding another's path. The wisdom I gained from my own challenges helped me develop a more compassionate understanding of manhood. I understood what being a dad is all about. I even understood Dana. I love my dad. Not because he was a perfect father to me, but simply because I choose to. No person needs a reason to love. You can love without qualification. And I don't always need validation for what I give in love. I give just because.

I counted out our relationship and I'm proud to say I was wrong.

What I predicted as taking a traumatic risk turned out to be my emotional liberation. I no longer need to receive a certain type of love from Dana, my mom, or anyone else to feel a sense of wholeness. I am whole because I choose to be.

We can all be adored, uplifted, famous, or important. We can be unified, vulnerable, courageous, and wise. We can be leaders, social changers, innovators, and power players. We can be anything and do anything. But no matter who we are or what we do, having love in our lives is essential.

When I was in my darkest days of despair, I was encouraged by love to believe in my purpose and trust my voice. When I was hurting, it was love that taught me the value of my time and the power I had to heal my life. Love always said to me, "Look ahead, better is coming." Love is never the thing pulling me down. Love has always lifted me up, boosted my esteem, confidence, sense of belonging, and purpose.

Love is really all that matters.

Love is the piece that makes us whole. It is the force that brings and keeps all good things together.

Love is why I'm proud to say, this is me.

ACKNOWLEDGMENTS

To my parents, family, and friends: Thank you for your support and encouragement throughout this book-writing process. I love you and I *know* I am loved by all of you (especially you, Mom).

To my big sister Elise: Thank you for all that you do. The convos, rides to the airport, nephew time, and all of the laughter we share. I love you.

To Jas Waters: When I called on you for guidance, I was about to call it quits and leave the book unfinished. Looking back on my life felt dizzying. Deciding what should or shouldn't be shared was overwhelming. But you helped me to find clarity. The phone conversations and the meet-ups were all very necessary. It was your listening and gentle reminders to keep writing that helped me to break through. Thank you, my friend.

To Todd Hunter: Thank you for helping me make this book happen. You believed in me as an author. The opportunity to write this book has been a dream come true. It was a longer process than either of us expected, but we got it done. Now let's do another!

To Nena Madonia and Dupree Miller Associates: Thank you!

To Atria Books: Thank you!

To my readers: My relationship with you has helped me to grow, and find joy and love. Over the years I've shared with you many intimate sides of myself, and, in turn, you've helped me reach a point where I don't want to hold back any longer. I want to give all of myself to my purpose. Thank you for helping me commit to that decision. Thank you for reading my books. Live bold. Choose to discover, unlock, and reveal all of that magnificence inside you.